# Biblical Coaching:

# Integrating Mental Health and Spiritual

# Growth

Published by Youth Success Coaching, LLC.

Fort Myers, Florida, USA

ISBN: 979-8-9875023-5-8 (Paperback)

www.youthsuccesscoaching.org

# Author

Sheryl Ellis is a mental health therapist, youth life coach, mentor, writer, and author of Christian-based books and curricula for youth. With over a decade of therapeutic youth services, Sheryl has a voice that shines through in her newest collection of books, exploring the importance of youth social and emotional wellness. Sheryl has a BA in Psychology and an MA in marriage and family counseling and is currently completing a PH. D in Developmental Psychology. Sheryl is a certified (TF-CBT) Trauma Focused Cognitive Behavioral Therapist working in schools, hospitals, and behavioral health centers, providing therapy for severely at-risk youth and teens. When not providing therapeutic services, Sheryl loves cooking, swimming, mountain bike riding, camping, and spending time with her family.

# Table of Contents

# Introduction

## About Biblical Coaching: Integrating Mental Health and

## Spiritual Growth

I am thrilled to introduce "*Biblical Coaching: Integrating Mental Health and Spiritual Growth*," a Coaching Course. As parents, guardians, and trusted adults, you are entrusted with the incredible responsibility of guiding the youth in your care. In today's world, young people face overwhelming challenges—social pressures, academic stress, and personal struggles—and knowing how to help them build the tools they need to cope and thrive can be difficult. Our *self-paced, faith-based* course on *Life Purpose, Empowerment, Resiliency, and Coping Skills* is here to provide the guidance you need, all rooted in biblical principles.

## Overview:

" *Biblical Coaching* " This comprehensive 8-week program is designed to help you guide youth to tap into their inner strength, discover their God-given purpose, and develop resilience rooted in faith. With every lesson, scripture-based teachings are intertwined with practical exercises to build essential coping skills. These are the Bible's life lessons and spiritual tools to foster personal growth, emotional fortitude, and spiritual maturity.

A well-structured *teaching manual* accompanies the three programs, ensuring you have everything you need to lead youth through lessons grounded in faith and scripture confidently. You'll walk alongside them as they learn to apply biblical truths to their lives, from understanding their purpose to building resilience and overcoming adversity.

The focus planner covers the following key areas:

1. **Universal Teaching Manual:** designed to guide parents, guardians, and trusted adults in helping youth.
2. The youth will be introduced to fundamental concepts such as the *Stages of Change* and *Love Languages in the early weeks. These will help* them understand how God works during transformation and deepen their emotional and spiritual connections with others. You'll also help them develop a *Growth Mindset*, showing them how Scripture encourages us to view challenges as opportunities to grow in faith and character.
3. **As the course progresses**, you'll guide them through powerful gratitude practices—drawing from biblical teachings on thankfulness. Youth will engage in daily *Gratitude Exercises* and keep a *Gratitude Journal*, helping them reflect on God's blessings and fostering a mindset of resilience through gratitude, just as the Bible instructs us to give thanks in all circumstances (1 Thessalonians 5:18).
4. **In later weeks**, youth will explore their past, present, and future narratives while learning to visualize their *Best Possible Self*, grounded in God's vision for their lives. Whether they are imagining their role within their family, school, or community,

these exercises will help them shape their identity and align their life goals with their faith.

5. **Finally**, the course culminates in *goal-setting activities* where youth learn to create *SMART Goals* (Specific, Measurable, Achievable, Relevant, Time-bound). These goals are rooted in the understanding that they fulfill God's plan for their lives, helping them confidently step into their purpose with divine guidance. You'll guide them in setting short-term and long-term goals, ensuring they have a faith-driven action plan to pursue their dreams.

But this course goes beyond helping youth cope—it empowers them to thrive by embracing their God-given strengths, clarifying their life's vision, and taking purposeful action in faith. You will also learn how to support them in building critical support systems—from family to their broader faith community—helping them grow in fellowship with others and remain grounded in God's truth.

With actionable tasks, biblical examples, and an emphasis on personal and spiritual growth, this course ensures you are fully equipped to help youth overcome adversity, build resilience, and unlock their full potential in Christ.

Transform how you support the young people in your life today—these *faith-based programs* will provide everything you need to ensure they emerge stronger in faith, more focused, and ready to thrive with a more profound sense of their unique, God-given purpose. Whether you're guiding a child, adolescent, or teen, this program will empower you to make a lasting, meaningful impact rooted in the teachings of the Bible.

Thank you for considering " ***Biblical Coaching***: *Integrating Mental Health and Spiritual Growth*." Together, let's make a difference in the lives of our children.

**Key Note:**

Any references to historical events, real people, or places are fictitious. Names, characters, and places are products of the author's imagination. Brief Scripture quotations marked KJV are from the King James Version(R). (1989-2022) Olive Tree Bible Reader Software, Inc. Spokane, WA: Olive Tree.

# Biblical Life Purpose Course Manual

## Course Overview

Welcome to the Biblical Life Purpose Course. This self-paced course is designed for parents, guardians, and trusted adults to guide youth in discovering and fulfilling their God-given purpose. By focusing on various elements, including God's Word, Jesus' teachings, the Holy Spirit, the Full Body of Armor, God's Angels, Brothers and Sisters in Christ, and the stages of change, participants will learn to help youth understand their chosen calling and develop their strengths.

## Course Objectives

By the end of this course, participants will be able to:

1. Understand and teach the stages of change from a biblical perspective.
2. Help youth identify their passions, personality, strengths, and spiritual gifts.
3. Clarify the vision, calling, and purpose for the youth in their care.
4. Guide youth in creating a strategy for their life's mission, using personal strengths and the Full Body of Armor.
5. Assist youth in setting goals, taking action, and moving forward in their mission.
6. Identify and overcome both external and internal obstacles that youth may face.
7. Use biblical examples to illustrate the principles of biblical empowerment.

Weekly Introductions

Week 1: Awareness - The Stages of Change, Satisfaction Assessment, Circumstances, World Views, God's Word

Introduction:

Welcome to Week 1 of the Biblical Life Purpose course. This week, we will focus on the stages of change, how to assess satisfaction in various areas of life, understanding circumstances and world views, and grounding ourselves in God's Word. Understanding these foundational concepts will help youth navigate their journey of discovering and fulfilling their life purpose.

Example to Illustrate Concepts:

- Stages of Change: Discuss the story of Saul's transformation to Paul (Acts 9). Highlight the stages of his change from persecutor to apostle.
- Satisfaction Assessment: Use a satisfaction wheel to help youth rate different areas of their lives (e.g., spiritual life, relationships, academics) and discuss.
- World Views: Compare the worldview of Joseph's brothers in Genesis with Joseph's God-centered worldview and its impact on their lives.

Week 2: Awareness - Passions, Personality, Strengths, Spiritual Gifts & Chosen

Introduction:

In Week 2, we will delve into discovering passions, understanding personality, identifying strengths, recognizing spiritual gifts, and embracing the concept of being chosen by God. This awareness helps youth understand their unique design and how it aligns with God's purpose for their lives.

Example to Illustrate Concepts:

- Passions and Strengths: Discuss David's passion for music and his strength as a warrior (1 Samuel 16-17).
- Spiritual Gifts: Reflect on the gifts of the Holy Spirit listed in 1 Corinthians 12. Have youth identify which gifts they see in themselves.
- Chosen by God: Study Jeremiah 1:5 to understand how God decides individuals for specific purposes even before birth.

Week 3: Vision - Clarify the Vision, Calling, Purpose

Introduction:

Welcome to Week 3, where we will focus on clarifying vision, understanding calling, and defining purpose. These elements are crucial for youth as they seek to understand God's plan for their lives. By the end of this week, you will be able to guide youth in articulating their vision and calling clearly.

Example to Illustrate Concepts:

- Clarifying Vision: Examine the vision given to Moses at the burning bush (Exodus 3). Discuss how this vision clarified his purpose.
- Understanding Calling: Explore the calling of the disciples by Jesus (Matthew 4:18-22). Discuss how this calling transformed their lives.
- Defining Purpose: Use Esther's story (Esther 4:14) to highlight how understanding her purpose helped her take action to save her people.

Week 4: Vision - Moving with the Mission

Introduction:

In Week 4, we will move from vision to mission. Understanding how to translate vision and calling into actionable mission statements is critical. This week, we will explore how to create mission statements and take the first steps toward fulfilling them.

Example to Illustrate Concepts:

- Mission Statements: Create a mission statement inspired by Nehemiah's response to the news of Jerusalem's walls (Nehemiah 1-2).
- Taking Initial Steps: Discuss how Jesus began his public ministry after his baptism and temptation (Luke 4:14-21).

Week 5: Strategy and Action - Create a Strategy and personal Strength, Full Body of Armor

Introduction:

Welcome to Week 5, where we will focus on creating a strategy to achieve the mission, utilizing personal strengths, and putting on the Full Body of Armor. These tools and techniques will equip youth to face challenges and stay on course.

Example to Illustrate Concepts:

- Creating a Strategy: Analyze how Joshua strategized to take the city of Jericho (Joshua 6).
- Entire Body of Armor: Study Ephesians 6:10-18. Role-play scenarios where youth use different parts of the armor to address challenges (e.g., Shield of Faith to fend off doubts).

Week 6: Strategy and Action - Setting Goals, Taking Action, Moving the Process Forward & Commission

Introduction:

Week 6 will emphasize setting specific goals, taking actionable steps, and moving the process forward. We will also explore the commission concept and understand how God commissions us for His work. By the end of this week, youth will be ready to implement their plans with confidence.

Example to Illustrate Concepts:

- Setting Goals: Use the example of Paul's missionary journeys (Acts 13-21) to illustrate setting and achieving goals.
- Taking Action: Discuss how Ruth took action to provide for herself and Naomi (Ruth 2).
- God's Commission: Study the Great Commission given by Jesus in Matthew 28:18-20 and its implications for us today.

Week 7: Obstacles - External Barriers, Energy Drainers & Obedience

Introduction:

Welcome to Week 7. This week, we will identify external barriers and energy drainers that can impede progress. We will also stress the importance of obedience to God's Word to overcome these obstacles. Understanding and addressing these challenges will help youth stay focused and resilient.

Example to Illustrate Concepts:

- External Barriers: Discuss Nehemiah's challenges while rebuilding the wall, such as opposition from Sanballat and Tobiah (Nehemiah 4).
- Energy Drainers: Reflect on Elijah's experience of exhaustion and how God rejuvenated him (1 Kings 19).
- Obedience: Study the story of Jonah, emphasizing the consequences of disobedience and the blessings of returning to God's path (Book of Jonah).

Week 8: Obstacles - Internal Barriers and Getting Past the Barriers

Introduction:

In the final week, we will focus on internal barriers and strategies to overcome them. Internal barriers can be more challenging, often requiring deep personal and spiritual work. By understanding and addressing these internal challenges, youth can develop a robust and resilient character grounded in faith.

Example to Illustrate Concepts:

- Internal Barriers: Discuss Peter's internal struggle with fear and doubt when he walked on water (Matthew 14:28-31).
- Overcoming Internal Barriers: Study the transformation of Gideon from a fearful individual to a mighty warrior (Judges 6-7).
- Building Resilience: Reflect on Paul's words in 2 Corinthians 12:9-10 about finding strength in weakness through God's grace.

Conclusion

This course will be a transformative journey for youth and guiding adults. This structured approach will give participants the tools and insights to help youth discover and fulfill their God-given purpose. Remember, the key to success in this course is consistent reflection, application of biblical principles, and ongoing support and encouragement. May God bless you and guide you in this critical mission

# Biblical Life Purpose Course

## Course Overview

This self-paced course on Biblical Life Purpose is designed for parents, guardians, and trusted adults to guide youth in discovering and fulfilling their God-given purpose. By focusing on God's Word, Jesus' teachings, the Holy Spirit, the Full Body of Armor, God's Angels, Brothers and Sisters in Christ, and the stages of change, participants will learn to help youth understand their chosen calling and develop their strengths.

## Course Objectives

By the end of this course, participants will be able to:

1. Understand and teach the stages of change from a biblical perspective.
2. Help youth identify their passions, personality, strengths, and spiritual gifts.
3. Clarify the vision, calling, and purpose for the youth in their care.
4. Guide youth in creating a strategy for their life's mission, using personal strengths and the Full Body of Armor.
5. Assist youth in setting goals, taking action, and moving forward in their mission.
6. Identify and overcome both external and internal obstacles that youth may face.
7. Use biblical examples to illustrate the principles of biblical empowerment.

Weekly Introductions

Week 1: Awareness - The Stages of Change, Satisfaction Assessment, Circumstances, World Views, God's Word

Introduction: Welcome to Week 1 of the Biblical Life Purpose course. This week, we will focus on the stages of change, how to assess satisfaction in various areas of life, understanding circumstances and world views, and grounding ourselves in God's Word. Understanding these foundational concepts will help youth navigate their journey of discovering and fulfilling their life purpose.

Week 2: Awareness - Passions, Personality, Strengths, Spiritual Gifts & Chosen

Introduction: In Week 2, we will delve into discovering passions, understanding personality, identifying strengths, recognizing spiritual gifts, and embracing the concept of being chosen by God. This awareness helps youth understand their unique design and how it aligns with God's purpose for their lives.

Week 3: Vision - Clarify the Vision, Calling, Purpose

Introduction: Welcome to Week 3, where we will focus on clarifying vision, understanding calling, and defining purpose. These elements are crucial for youth as they seek to understand God's plan for their lives. By the end of this week, you will be able to guide youth in articulating their vision and calling clearly.

Week 4: Vision - Moving with the Mission

Introduction: In Week 4, we will move from vision to mission. Understanding how to translate vision and calling into actionable mission statements is critical. This week, we will explore how to create mission statements and take the first steps toward fulfilling them.

Week 5: Strategy and Action - Create a Strategy & Personal Strength, Full Body of Armor

Introduction: Welcome to Week 5, where we will focus on creating a strategy to achieve the mission, utilizing personal strengths, and putting on the Full Body of Armor. These tools and techniques will equip youth to face challenges and stay on course.

Week 6: Strategy and Action - Setting Goals, Taking Action, Moving the Process Forward & Commission

Introduction: In Week 6, we will emphasize setting specific goals, taking actionable steps, and moving the process forward. We will also explore the commission concept and understand how God commissions us for His work. By the end of this week, youth will be ready to implement their plans with confidence.

Week 7: Obstacles - External Barriers, Energy Drainers & Obedience

Introduction: Welcome to Week 7. This week, we will identify external barriers and energy drainers that can impede progress. We will also stress the importance of obedience to God's Word to overcome these obstacles. Understanding and addressing these challenges will help youth stay focused and resilient.

Week 8: Obstacles - Internal Barriers and Getting Past the Barriers

Introduction: In the final week, we will focus on internal barriers and strategies to overcome them. Internal barriers can be more challenging, often requiring deep personal and spiritual work. By understanding and addressing these internal challenges, youth can develop a robust and resilient character grounded in faith.

# Biblical Example of Empowerment

Name: Joseph

1. Story Overview:
   - Joseph, the son of Jacob, was sold into slavery by his brothers but rose to become the second most powerful man in Egypt. His story is a profound example of God's purpose unfolding through trials and triumphs.
2. Experiences:
   - Joseph experienced betrayal, slavery, false accusations, and imprisonment. Despite these hardships, he remained faithful to God and used his leadership and dream interpretation gifts.
3. Spiritual Connection and Overcoming Barriers:
   - Joseph's unwavering faith in God helped him interpret dreams and provide wise counsel, eventually leading to his rise in power. His ability to forgive his brothers and see God's plan exemplifies overcoming internal and external barriers.
4. The Role of the Devil:
   - The adversities Joseph faced, including the temptation by Potiphar's wife and the betrayal by his brothers, can be seen as works of the Devil aimed at derailing God's plan.
5. Combating Through Prayer and Scriptures (KJV Only):

- Joseph's story highlights the importance of trusting in God's promises: "But as for you, ye thought evil against me; but God meant it unto good, to bring to pass, as it is this day, to save many people alive." (Genesis 50:20 KJV)
- Prayer: Encourage youth to pray for strength and wisdom as Joseph did, seeking God's guidance in all circumstances.

Conclusion

Throughout this course, we have explored various aspects of discovering and fulfilling a biblical life purpose. By focusing on awareness, vision, strategy, action, and overcoming obstacles, you are now equipped to guide youth in their journey of understanding and living out their God-given purpose. Continue to support and mentor them with faith, love, and the wisdom of God's Word. Remember, God chooses each young person for a unique purpose; your role is to help them realize and achieve it with confidence and faith.

Week 1: Awareness - The Stages of Change, Satisfaction Assessment, Circumstances, World Views, God's Word

Introduction

Welcome to Week 1 of our course on Biblical Life Purpose. This week, we will lay the foundation by exploring the stages of change, conducting a satisfaction assessment, understanding circumstances, examining world views, and emphasizing the importance of grounding ourselves in God's Word. These elements are essential for understanding where we are spiritually, emotionally, and personally and how God's Word provides guidance and perspective in discovering our life's purpose.

The Stages of Change

Understanding the Stages

1. Pre-contemplation
   ○ Recognizing the need for change and openness to exploring God's purpose.
   ○ Scripture: "The Lord is not slack concerning his promise, as some men count slackness; but is longsuffering to us-ward, not willing that any should perish, but that all should come to repentance." (2 Peter 3:9 KJV)
2. Contemplation
   ○ I reflected on personal circumstances and considered how God's Word can provide direction.

- Scripture: "Thy word is a lamp unto my feet and a light unto my path." (Psalm 119:105 KJV)
3. Preparation
     - Preparing oneself mentally, emotionally, and spiritually to seek God's purpose.
     - Scripture: "Commit thy works unto the Lord, and thy thoughts shall be established." (Proverbs 16:3 KJV)
4. Action
     - Taking concrete steps to align with God's Word and seek His purpose.
     - Scripture: "I press toward the mark for the prize of the high calling of God in Christ Jesus." (Philippians 3:14 KJV)
5. Maintenance
     - Sustaining progress through continual prayer, study of God's Word, and seeking His guidance.
     - Scripture: "And let us not be weary in well doing: for in due season we shall reap if we faint not." (Galatians 6:9 KJV)

Satisfaction Assessment

Evaluating Satisfaction

1. Reflecting on Life Areas
     - We assess spiritual, relational, professional, and personal satisfaction.
     - Scripture: "But seek ye first the kingdom of God, and his righteousness; and all these

things shall be added unto you." (Matthew 6:33 KJV)

2. Seeking God's Guidance
   - o I am inviting God into the assessment process to reveal areas for growth and change.
   - o Scripture: "Trust in the Lord with all thine heart, and lean not unto thine own understanding. In all thy ways acknowledge him, and he shall direct thy paths." (Proverbs 3:5-6 KJV)

Circumstances

Understanding Circumstances

1. God's Sovereignty
   - o Recognizing that God works through all circumstances for His purpose.
   - o Scripture: "And we know that all things work together for good to them that love God, to them who are the called according to his purpose." (Romans 8:28 KJV)
2. Trusting God's Plan
   - o They trust that even challenging circumstances can be opportunities for growth and alignment with God's will.
   - o Scripture: "For I know the thoughts that I think toward you, saith the Lord, thoughts of peace, and not of evil, to give you an expected end." (Jeremiah 29:11 KJV)

World Views

Examining World Views

1. Biblical Perspective
    o We are understanding how God's Word shapes our worldview and understanding of life's purpose.
    o Scripture: "And be not conformed to this world: but be ye transformed by the renewing of your mind, that ye may prove what is that good, and acceptable, and perfect, will of God." (Romans 12:2 KJV)
2. Discerning Truth
    o Discerning truth from worldly perspectives through the lens of Scripture.
    o Scripture: "Buy the truth, and sell it not; also wisdom, and instruction, and understanding." (Proverbs 23:23 KJV)

God's Word

Grounded in God's Word

1. Source of Truth
    o They understand the Bible as the ultimate source of truth and guidance for life.
    o Scripture: "All scripture is given by inspiration of God, and is profitable for doctrine, for reproof, for correction, for instruction in righteousness." (2 Timothy 3:16 KJV)

2. Application in Daily Life
    o We are applying God's Word practically to navigate life's challenges and discover purpose.
    o Scripture: "Thy word have I hid in mine heart, that I might not sin against thee." (Psalm 119:11 KJV)

Conclusion

This week, you have laid the groundwork for discovering and fulfilling your biblical life purpose by exploring the stages of change, conducting a satisfaction assessment, understanding circumstances, examining world views, and grounding yourself in God's Word. As you continue this course, remember to seek God's guidance in every step, trusting His plan and purpose for your life. Next week, we will delve deeper into understanding passions, personality, strengths, and spiritual gifts as essential elements in discerning God's calling.

Week 2: Awareness - Passions, Personality, Strengths, Spiritual Gifts & Chosen

Introduction

Welcome to Week 2 of our Biblical Life Purpose course. This week, we will explore essential aspects of understanding oneself in God's plan: passions, personality, strengths, spiritual gifts, and the concept of being chosen by God. These elements are foundational in discovering how God has uniquely designed each person for a specific purpose and calling.

Passions

Discovering Passions

1. Identifying What Ignites You
    ○ Reflecting on activities or causes that bring joy and fulfillment.
    ○ Scripture: "Delight thyself also in the Lord, and he shall give thee the desires of thine heart." (Psalm 37:4 KJV)
2. Aligning Passions with God's Will
    ○ They consider how passions can align with God's purposes and kingdom principles.
    ○ Scripture: "Commit thy way unto the Lord; trust also in him; and he shall bring it to pass." (Psalm 37:5 KJV)

Personality

Understanding Personality

1. Personality Assessments
   - ○ I am exploring different personality types and traits to understand strengths and weaknesses.
   - ○ Scripture: "I can do all things through Christ which strengtheneth me." (Philippians 4:13 KJV)
2. God's Design in Personality
   - ○ He recognizes that God has uniquely fashioned each person's personality for His purposes.
   - ○ Scripture: "For thou hast possessed my reins: thou hast covered me in my mother's womb. I will praise thee; for I am fearfully and wonderfully made: marvelous are thy works; and that my soul knoweth right well." (Psalm 139:13-14 KJV)

Strengths

Identifying Strengths

1. Strengths Assessment
   - ○ Evaluating personal strengths, skills, and abilities.
   - ○ Scripture: "And whatsoever ye do, do it heartily, as to the Lord, and not unto men;" (Colossians 3:23 KJV)
2. Using Strengths for God's Glory

- Understanding how strengths can be used to serve God and others.
- Scripture: "As every man hath received the gift, even so, minister the same one to another, as good stewards of the manifold grace of God." (1 Peter 4:10 KJV)

Spiritual Gifts

Recognizing Spiritual Gifts

1. Gifts Assessment
   - I am discovering spiritual gifts through prayer, study, and community affirmation.
   - Scripture: "Now there are diversities of gifts, but the same Spirit." (1 Corinthians 12:4 KJV)
2. Using Gifts in Ministry
   - I am using spiritual gifts to build up the body of Christ and fulfill God's purposes.
   - Scripture: "As every man hath received the gift, even so, minister the same one to another, as good stewards of the manifold grace of God." (1 Peter 4:10 KJV)

Chosen

Understanding Being Chosen

1. God's Election
   - Reflecting on God's sovereign choice and calling of individuals.

- o Scripture: "But ye are a chosen generation, a royal priesthood, a holy nation, a peculiar people; that ye should shew forth the praises of him who hath called you out of darkness into his marvelous light." (1 Peter 2:9 KJV)
2. Living Out God's Calling
   - o I am embracing the privilege and responsibility of being chosen to serve God's kingdom purposes.
   - o Scripture: "For many are called, but few are chosen." (Matthew 22:14 KJV)

Conclusion

This week, you have explored passions, personality, strengths, spiritual gifts, and the concept of being chosen by God. These elements are integral in understanding how God has uniquely equipped and called each individual for a specific purpose. As you continue this course, reflect on these insights and seek God's guidance to discern how to align your passions, utilize your strengths, and live out your calling for His glory. Next week, we will clarify vision, calling, and purpose, building upon the foundational awareness gained in Weeks 1 and 2.

Week 3: Vision - Clarify the Vision, Calling, Purpose

Introduction

Welcome to Week 3 of our Biblical Life Purpose course. This week, we embark on a journey to clarify the vision, understand calling, and define purpose in God's divine plan for your life. These foundational elements will guide you in aligning your goals and actions with God's will, ensuring you walk confidently in the path He has set.

Clarifying the Vision

Defining Your Vision

1. Vision Statement
   o A vision statement outlines your aspirations and goals for the future, reflecting God's purpose for your life.
   o Scripture: "Write the vision, and make it plain upon tables, that he may run that readeth it." (Habakkuk 2:2 KJV)
2. Seeking Divine Guidance
   o Seek God's wisdom and guidance through prayer and meditation to clarify your vision.
   o Scripture: "Commit thy works unto the Lord, and thy thoughts shall be established." (Proverbs 16:3 KJV)
3. Aligning with Kingdom Purposes
   o Ensure that your vision aligns with God's kingdom's purposes and brings glory to Him.

- Scripture: "But seek ye first the kingdom of God, and his righteousness; and all these things shall be added unto you." (Matthew 6:33 KJV)

Understanding Calling

Discerning Your Calling

1. Listening to God's Voice
   - Cultivate a listening heart to discern God's calling through prayer, Scripture, and quiet reflection.
   - Scripture: "And thine ears shall hear a word behind thee, saying, This is the way, walk ye in it, when ye turn to the right hand, and when ye turn to the left." (Isaiah 30:21 KJV)
2. Confirming Through Confirmation
   - Seek confirmation from mentors, spiritual leaders, and the community of believers to affirm your calling.
   - Scripture: "Wherefore, brethren, look ye out among you seven men of honest report, full of the Holy Ghost and wisdom, whom we may appoint over this business." (Acts 6:3 KJV)
3. Obedience to God's Call
   - Embrace obedience to God's call, trusting His sovereignty and faithfulness to equip you.
   - Scripture: "And Samuel said, Hath the Lord as great delight in burnt offerings and sacrifices, as in obeying the voice of the

Lord? Behold, to obey is better than sacrifice, and to hearken than the fat of rams." (1 Samuel 15:22 KJV)

Defining Purpose

Articulating Your Purpose

1. Purpose Statement
   o Craft a purpose statement articulating why God created you and how He intends to use your life for His glory.
   o Scripture: "For we are his workmanship, created in Christ Jesus unto good works, which God hath before ordained that we should walk in them." (Ephesians 2:10 KJV)
2. Living Out God's Purpose
   o Intentionally live out your purpose by aligning your actions with God's Word and His leading.
   o Scripture: "And whatsoever ye do in word or deed, do all in the name of the Lord Jesus, giving thanks to God and the Father by him." (Colossians 3:17 KJV)

Exercise: Writing Your Vision, Calling, and Purpose

1. Reflection Time
   o Set aside dedicated time for prayer and reflection to write down your vision, calling, and purpose statements.
2. Seek Feedback

o Share your statements with a trusted mentor, spiritual advisor, or fellow believers for feedback and encouragement.

Conclusion

This week, you have embarked on the journey to clarify your vision, understand your calling, and define your purpose within God's divine plan. As you continue this course, seek God's guidance diligently, trusting that He who began a good work in you will complete it. Your vision, calling, and purpose are pivotal in fulfilling God's mission for your life and impacting His kingdom. Next week, we will explore practical strategies for moving forward with your mission, building upon the foundational clarity gained in Week 3.

Week 4: Vision - Moving with the Mission

Introduction

Welcome to Week 4 of our Biblical Life Purpose course. This week, we transition from the foundational work of clarifying your vision, calling, and purpose to actively moving with the mission that God has entrusted to you. This phase is pivotal as it involves practical steps, intentional actions, and spiritual alignment to effectively fulfill God's purposes for your life. By the end of this week, you will gain insights into how to move forward purposefully, leveraging your strengths and spiritual gifts to impact the world for Christ.

Embracing Your Mission

Understanding Your Role

1. Identity in Christ
   - Your identity as a child of God is foundational to understanding your mission. You are chosen and set apart by God for His purposes.
   - Scripture: "But ye are a chosen generation, a royal priesthood, a holy nation, a peculiar people; that ye should shew forth the praises of him who hath called you out of darkness into his marvelous light." (1 Peter 2:9 KJV)
   - Reflect on what it means to be chosen by God. Consider how your identity in Christ shapes your perspective on fulfilling His mission.

2. Servant Leadership
   o Jesus exemplified servant leadership throughout His ministry. He came not to be served but to serve and give His life as a ransom for many.
   o Scripture: "For even the Son of man came not to be ministered unto, but to minister, and to give his life a ransom for many." (Mark 10:45 KJV)
   o How can you adopt the mindset of servant leadership in your mission? Reflect on ways to serve others and advance God's kingdom with humility and compassion.

Aligning with God's Will

Seeking Divine Guidance

1. Prayer and Seeking Wisdom
   o Prayer is essential in discerning and aligning with God's will for your mission. Ask God for wisdom and clarity as you seek to fulfill His purposes.
   o Scripture: "If any of you lack wisdom, let him ask of God, that giveth to all men liberally, and upbraideth not; and it shall be given him." (James 1:5 KJV)
   o Spend dedicated time in prayer this week, seeking God's guidance on specific aspects of your mission. Listen attentively to His voice through Scripture and prayer.
2. Obeying God's Commands

- Obedience is crucial in walking out your mission. Trust that God's commands are for your good and His glory.
- Scripture: "And be not conformed to this world: but be ye transformed by the renewing of your mind, that ye may prove what is that good, and acceptable, and perfect, will of God." (Romans 12:2 KJV)
- Reflect on areas where obedience to God's commands is challenging. How can you align your actions more closely with His Word and will?

Taking Action

Steps Towards Your Mission

1. Setting Strategic Goals
   - Strategic goal-setting helps translate your vision into actionable steps. Set SMART goals (Specific, Measurable, Achievable, Relevant, Time-bound) that align with your mission.
   - Scripture: "Commit thy works unto the Lord, and thy thoughts shall be established." (Proverbs 16:3 KJV)
   - Take time this week to outline specific goals related to your mission. Consider how each goal contributes to fulfilling God's purposes.
2. Being Diligent and Persistent
   - Diligence and persistence are virtues in pursuing your mission. Trust in God's

faithfulness and persevere in the face of challenges.

○ Scripture: "And let us not be weary in well doing: for in due season we shall reap if we faint not." (Galatians 6:9 KJV)

○ Reflect on moments when perseverance was crucial in your journey. How can you cultivate a spirit of perseverance as you pursue God's mission for your life?

Exercise: Mapping Your Mission Journey

1. Reflection and Planning
   ○ Set aside time to reflect on your vision, calling, and purpose statements. Map out practical steps and milestones that will lead you closer to fulfilling your mission.
   ○ Scripture: "For which of you, intending to build a tower, sitteth not down first, and counteth the cost, whether he have sufficient to finish it?" (Luke 14:28 KJV)
   ○ Consider the resources, skills, and support needed to accomplish each step of your mission journey.

2. Seek Divine Confirmation
   ○ Seek divine confirmation through prayer and seeking counsel from mature believers. Share your mission journey with trusted mentors who can provide guidance and accountability.
   ○ Scripture: "Where no counsel is, the people fall: but in the multitude of counselors there is safety." (Proverbs 11:14 KJV)

- How can seeking counsel from others strengthen your mission journey? Reflect on the importance of community and accountability in fulfilling God's purposes.

Conclusion

This week, you have embarked on the critical moving phase with the mission God entrusted you with. By embracing your identity in Christ, aligning with God's will through prayer and obedience, and taking intentional steps toward your mission goals, you are positioning yourself to impact the world for Christ's glory. As you continue this course, remain steadfast in your commitment to follow God's leading and faithfully serve His kingdom. Next week, we will explore practical strategies for effectively leveraging your strengths and spiritual gifts to implement your mission.

Week 5: Strategy and Action - Create a Strategy &
Personal Strength, Full Body of Armor

Introduction

Welcome to Week 5 of our Biblical Life Purpose course.
This week, we will focus on creating a strategic plan for
your mission and delving deeper into the spiritual
empowerment provided by the whole armor of God.
Understanding and applying these principles will
strengthen your resolve and equip you to overcome
obstacles as you pursue God's call on your life.

Creating a Strategy

Developing Your Strategic Plan

1. Identifying Goals and Objectives
   o Review and refine your mission and vision
     statements in light of God's Word. Clarify
     specific goals and objectives that align with
     His kingdom's purposes.
   o Scripture: "Commit thy works unto the
     Lord, and thy thoughts shall be established."
     (Proverbs 16:3 KJV)
   o Reflect on how God's Word shapes your
     goals. How can your plans reflect His glory
     and serve His kingdom?
2. Mapping Out Action Steps
   o Break down each goal into actionable steps
     with clear timelines and measurable
     outcomes. Seek accountability from trusted
     mentors or peers.

- Scripture: "The heart of man plans his way, but the Lord establishes his steps." (Proverbs 16:9 KJV)
- Consider how prayer and seeking God's guidance can be integrated into your strategic planning. How can you ensure each step aligns with His will?

Leveraging Personal Strengths and the Full Armor of God

Recognizing and Utilizing Your Strengths

1. Strengths Assessment
   - Begin by acknowledging that God has uniquely gifted each believer with specific talents and abilities for His kingdom's purposes.
   - Scripture: "For I say, through the grace given unto me, to every man that is among you, not to think of himself more highly than he ought to think; but to think soberly, according as God hath dealt to every man the measure of faith." (Romans 12:3 KJV)
   - Reflect on Romans 12:3, which reminds us to humbly recognize our strengths as gifts from God, intended for serving others and glorifying His name.
2. Using Spiritual Gifts
   - Identify and actively use your spiritual gifts to build up the body of Christ and fulfill your mission.
   - **Scripture**: "Having then gifts differing according to the grace that is given to us,

whether prophecy, let us prophesy according to the proportion of faith;" (Romans 12:6 KJV)

- o Consider how Paul encourages believers in Romans 12:6 to use their spiritual gifts according to the grace given them, emphasizing the importance of stewarding these gifts faithfully in service to God's kingdom.

The Full Armor of God: A Biblical Perspective

1. Understanding Spiritual Warfare
   - o Recognize that, as believers, we are engaged in a spiritual battle against forces of darkness and spiritual wickedness.
   - o Scripture: "For we wrestle not against flesh and blood, but against principalities, against powers, against the rulers of the darkness of this world, against spiritual wickedness in high places." (Ephesians 6:12 KJV)
   - o Ephesians 6:12 provides a clear understanding of the spiritual warfare we face, highlighting the importance of being spiritually equipped to stand firm against the schemes of the devil.
2. Putting on the Full Armor of God
   - o Paul's analogy of the armor of God in Ephesians 6:13-18 illustrates essential spiritual qualities and disciplines necessary for victorious Christian living.
   - o Scripture: "Wherefore take unto you the whole armor of God, that ye may be able to

withstand in the evil day, and having done all, to stand." (Ephesians 6:13 KJV)

o Each piece of armor represents a spiritual principle or practice that equips believers to withstand spiritual attacks and live victoriously in Christ.

o The Belt of Truth: This foundational piece holds the armor together, representing the truth of God's Word that guides our beliefs and actions (Ephesians 6:14).

o The Breastplate of Righteousness: Protecting the heart symbolizes living a righteous life, obeying God's commands, and guarding against spiritual attacks (Ephesians 6:14).

o The Gospel of Peace: Footwear that equips believers to stand firm and bring the message of reconciliation and peace through Christ to the world (Ephesians 6:15).

o The Shield of Faith: A shield that protects against the fiery darts of doubt and fear, strengthened by unwavering trust in God's promises and power (Ephesians 6:16).

o The Helmet of Salvation: Protecting the mind, the helmet represents the assurance of salvation and the hope of eternal life in Christ, guarding against doubts and spiritual attacks on our identity in Christ (Ephesians 6:17).

o The Sword of the Spirit is the Word of God: The offensive weapon of prayerful proclamation and application of God's

Word, defeating spiritual strongholds and lies with truth (Ephesians 6:17).

- o Prayer in the Spirit: Continuous communication with God through prayer, seeking His wisdom, guidance, and empowerment in all circumstances (Ephesians 6:18).

Exercise: Developing Your Strategy and Strengthening Your Armor

1. Strategic Planning Session
   - o Set aside time to develop or refine your strategic plan to fulfill your mission. Seek input from spiritual mentors or peers for valuable insights.
2. Personal Reflection and Application
   - o Reflect on how you can leverage your strengths and the whole armor of God to overcome challenges and advance confidently in your mission. Consider specific areas where you need to grow in utilizing your spiritual gifts and applying the principles of the armor of God.

Conclusion

This week, you have explored the biblical principles of leveraging personal strengths and spiritual empowerment through the whole armor of God. By recognizing and stewarding your strengths as gifts from God and by actively putting on the whole armor of God to engage in spiritual warfare, you are equipping yourself to fulfill God's call on your life effectively. As you continue this course, maintain a posture of humility, prayer, and dependence on the Holy Spirit's guidance. Next week, we will delve into practical strategies for setting goals, taking action, and advancing in alignment with God's will, building upon the foundational clarity gained in Week 5.

Week 6: Strategy and Action - Setting Goals, Taking Action, Moving the Process Forward & Commission

Introduction

Welcome to Week 6 of our Biblical Life Purpose course. This week, we focus on practical strategies for setting goals, taking intentional action, and confidently fulfilling God's call on your life. Additionally, we will explore the concept of commissioning, where believers are entrusted with specific tasks or missions by God to impact the world for His glory.

Setting Goals

Principles of Goal Setting

1. Aligning Goals with God's Will
   o Begin by seeking God's guidance through prayer and Scripture to discern goals that align with His purposes.
   o Scripture: "Commit thy way unto the Lord; trust also in him; and he shall bring it to pass." (Psalm 37:5 KJV)
   o Reflect on Psalm 37:5, which encourages us to commit our plans to the Lord, trusting Him to guide and fulfill His purposes through us.

SMART Goals

Utilizing the SMART Criteria

1. Specific
   - Ensure your goals are specific and clearly defined. Avoid vague objectives that can lead to ambiguity and lack of focus.
   - Scripture: "Commit thy works unto the Lord, and thy thoughts shall be established." (Proverbs 16:3 KJV)
   - Proverbs 16:3 encourages us to commit our plans to the Lord, implying clarity and specificity in our actions. How can you align your goals with God's specific purposes for your life?
2. Measurable
   - Set criteria to measure progress and success. Define metrics that allow you to track your advancement towards achieving your goals.
   - Scripture: "The plans of the diligent lead surely to abundance, but everyone who is hasty comes only to poverty." (Proverbs 21:5 KJV)
   - Reflect on Proverbs 21:5, which underscores the importance of diligence and measurement in achieving success. How can you establish measurable indicators for your goals?
3. Achievable
   - Ensure your goals are realistic and attainable within the resources and time frame.

- o Scripture: "I can do all things through Christ which strengtheneth me." (Philippians 4:13 KJV)
- o Philippians 4:13 reminds us of our dependence on Christ's strength to accomplish everything. How can you set goals that stretch your faith yet remain achievable through God's empowerment?

4. Relevant
- o Align your goals with your broader mission and vision. Ensure they contribute meaningfully to your overall purpose and calling.
- o Scripture: "And whatsoever ye do, do it heartily, as to the Lord, and not unto men;" (Colossians 3:23 KJV)
- o Colossians 3:23 emphasizes doing everything with wholehearted dedication to the Lord. How can you ensure your goals are relevant to God's kingdom purposes and glorify Him?

5. Time-bound
- o Establish a timeline for achieving your goals. Setting deadlines creates urgency and helps prioritize tasks effectively.
- o Scripture: "For ye need patience, that, after ye have done the will of God, ye might receive the promise." (Hebrews 10:36 KJV)
- o Hebrews 10:36 highlights the importance of patience in waiting for God's promises. How can you set realistic deadlines that honor God's timing while motivating diligent effort?

Reflection on Luke 14:28

Jesus' illustration of planning to build a tower in Luke 14:28 is a profound reminder of the wisdom in counting the cost before embarking on any significant endeavor. By applying this principle to your goal-setting process using the SMART criteria, you ensure that your goals are well-thought-out and aligned with God's will:

- Planning: Take deliberate steps to plan your goals, considering the resources, time, and effort required.
- Counting the Cost: Evaluate the sacrifices and commitments needed to achieve your goals, seeking God's guidance.
- Sufficiency: Trust in God's provision and strength to equip you adequately for the tasks He sets before you.

As you integrate Luke 14:28 with the SMART criteria, you cultivate a disciplined approach to goal-setting that honors God, maximizes your potential, and furthers His kingdom's purposes. Remember, your goals are not merely about personal achievement but glorifying God in all you do.

Taking Action

Implementing Your Action Plan

1. Initiating Action Steps
    o Break down each goal into smaller action steps and prioritize them based on their impact and alignment with your mission.

- Scripture: "Whatsoever thy hand findeth to do, do it with thy might; for there is no work, nor device, nor knowledge, nor wisdom, in the grave, whither thou goest." (Ecclesiastes 9:10 KJV)
- Reflect on Ecclesiastes 9:10, which encourages wholehearted dedication in carrying out tasks. How can you approach your action steps with diligence and commitment?

2. Overcoming Procrastination and Obstacles
   - Address potential obstacles or distractions that may hinder your progress. Stay resilient in pursuing God's purposes despite challenges.
   - Scripture: "I can do all things through Christ which strengtheneth me." (Philippians 4:13 KJV)
   - Draw strength from Philippians 4:13, affirming your ability to persevere and overcome obstacles through Christ's strength. How can this verse inspire your approach to overcoming challenges in your mission?

Moving the Process Forward

Advancing in Your Mission

1. Monitoring Progress
   - Regularly evaluate your progress towards goals and adjust to stay on track.

- Scripture: "Let us not be weary in well doing: for in due season we shall reap if we faint not." (Galatians 6:9 KJV)
- Reflect on Galatians 6:9, which encourages perseverance in doing good and trusting in God's timing for the harvest. How can this perspective sustain your motivation to advance your mission?

2. Seeking Divine Guidance
    - Continually seek God's guidance through prayer and meditation on His Word to navigate decisions and opportunities that arise.
    - Scripture: "Trust in the Lord with all thine heart, and lean not unto thine own understanding. In all thy ways acknowledge him, and he shall direct thy paths." (Proverbs 3:5-6 KJV)
    - Meditate on Proverbs 3:5-6, affirming the importance of trusting God's wisdom and guidance. How can you apply this principle when seeking direction for your mission?

Commission

Embracing Your Commission

1. Understanding Your God-given Commission
   - Reflect on how God has uniquely commissioned you to fulfill specific tasks or roles in His kingdom.
   - Scripture: "And he said unto them, Go ye into all the world, and preach the gospel to every creature." (Mark 16:15 KJV)
   - Consider Mark 16:15, where Jesus commissions His disciples to proclaim the gospel to all nations. How does this commission resonate with your sense of calling?

2. Living Out Your Mission
   - Embrace your commission with courage and faithfulness, knowing that God equips and empowers you for the tasks He assigns.
   - Scripture: "And whatsoever ye do, do it heartily, as to the Lord, and not unto men;" (Colossians 3:23 KJV)
   - Reflect on Colossians 3:23, which encourages wholehearted dedication to serving God. How can you approach your commission with a mindset of serving God above all else?

Exercise: Advancing Your Mission

1. Action Plan Review
   - Review and refine your action plan based on the principles discussed this week. Identify any adjustments needed to align more closely with God's will and your mission.
2. Prayer and Reflection
   - Spend intentional time in prayer, seeking God's guidance and strength as you take action and advance in fulfilling your mission.

Conclusion

This week, you have explored practical strategies for setting goals, taking action, and advancing confidently in fulfilling God's call on your life. By aligning your goals with God's will, taking intentional steps to implement your action plan, monitoring progress, and embracing your commission with faithfulness, you are positioning yourself to impact the world for Christ's glory. As you continue this course, maintain a posture of prayer, dependence on God's guidance, and perseverance in pursuing His purposes. Next week, we will explore overcoming external barriers and cultivating obedience to fulfill your life purpose.

Week 7: Obstacles - External Barriers, Energy Drainers & Obedience

Introduction

Welcome to Week 7 of our Biblical Life Purpose course. This week, we will address the obstacles hindering our progress in fulfilling God's call on our lives. We will focus on identifying and overcoming external barriers, managing energy drainers, and cultivating obedience to God's guidance amidst challenges.

External Barriers

Recognizing External Challenges

1. Identifying External Barriers
    o External barriers can include opposition from others, logistical challenges, financial constraints, or societal pressures.
    o Scripture: "The thief cometh not, but for to steal, and to kill, and to destroy: I come that they might have life and that they might have it more abundantly." (John 10:10 KJV)
    o Reflect on John 10:10, where Jesus acknowledges the reality of spiritual opposition. How can you discern between external challenges that distract from God's purpose and those that refine your faith?
2. Strategies for Overcoming
    o Seek God's wisdom and strength to navigate external barriers with faith and

perseverance. Utilize prayer, wise counsel, and strategic planning.

- Scripture: "I will instruct thee and teach thee in the way which thou shalt go: I will guide thee with mine eye." (Psalm 32:8 KJV)
- Meditate on Psalm 32:8, affirming God's promise to guide and instruct you. How can you apply His guidance in overcoming external obstacles?

Energy Drainers

Managing Spiritual and Physical Energy

1. Identifying Energy Drainers
   - Energy drainers can include negative influences, excessive busyness, lack of rest, or emotional stressors that deplete spiritual and physical vitality.
   - Scripture: "But they that wait upon the Lord shall renew their strength; they shall mount up with wings as eagles; they shall run, and not be weary; and they shall walk, and not faint." (Isaiah 40:31 KJV)
   - Reflect on Isaiah 40:31, which promises renewal and strength for those waiting for the Lord. How can you prioritize spiritual and physical rest to maintain energy for God's work?
2. Strategies for Restoration
   - Develop healthy habits of prayer, meditation on Scripture, Sabbath rest, and balanced

time management to combat energy drainers.

- o Scripture: "And he said unto me, My grace is sufficient for thee: for my strength is made perfect in weakness." (2 Corinthians 12:9 KJV)
- o Consider 2 Corinthians 12:9, where God assures His sufficiency in our weakness. How can you rely on His grace to replenish your energy and resilience?

Cultivating Obedience

Walking in God's Will

1. Understanding Obedience
   - o Obedience involves aligning your actions and decisions with God's Word and His leading, even when it contradicts worldly wisdom or personal desires.
   - o Scripture: "If ye love me, keep my commandments." (John 14:15 KJV)
   - o Reflect on John 14:15, where Jesus links love for Him with obedience to His commandments. How can you deepen your love for God through obedient living?
2. Challenges and Rewards
   - o Embrace the challenges of obedience, trusting in God's promises of blessings, and His faithfulness to fulfill His purposes through obedient hearts.
   - o Scripture: "And we know that all things work together for good to them that love

God, to them who are the called according to his purpose." (Romans 8:28 KJV)

- ○ Meditate on Romans 8:28, affirming God's sovereignty over all circumstances. How can you trust Him to turn obstacles into opportunities for His glory?

Exercise: Overcoming Obstacles

1. Obstacle Assessment
   - ○ Identify external barriers and energy drainers that have hindered your progress in fulfilling God's call. Prayerfully discern their origins and impact on your spiritual journey.
2. Prayer and Action
   - ○ Dedicate time to surrender these obstacles to God prayerfully, seeking His wisdom and strength to overcome them. Take intentional steps to address them with faith and perseverance.

Conclusion

In Week 7, you explored strategies for overcoming external barriers, managing energy drainers, and cultivating obedience in fulfilling God's call. By relying on God's guidance, renewing your strength through spiritual disciplines, and embracing obedience to His will, you can navigate challenges and remain steadfast in pursuing His purposes. As you continue this course, maintain a posture of dependence on God's grace and a commitment to obedience, trusting Him to lead you through every obstacle.

Next week, we will delve into overcoming internal barriers and growing in spiritual resilience, building upon the foundation laid in Week 7.

Week 8: Obstacles - Internal Barriers and Getting Past the Barriers

Introduction

Hey everyone, welcome to the final week of our Biblical Life Purpose course! This week, we will focus on the internal barriers that can hold us back from fully living out God's plan for our lives. We'll explore how to identify and overcome these obstacles to move forward confidently in our faith journey.

Internal Barriers

Identifying Internal Challenges

Internal barriers are the things within ourselves—like doubts, fears, or negative thoughts—that can make it hard to follow God's calling.

- Scripture: "For God gave us a spirit not of fear but of power and love and self-control." (2 Timothy 1:7 KJV)

This verse reminds us that God has given us the power to overcome our fears and doubts through His Spirit. How can we rely on His strength to face our internal struggles?

Overcoming Doubts and Fears

1. Replacing Lies with Truth
   - Combat negative thoughts and lies with God's truth found in Scripture. Meditate on verses that affirm God's promises and His faithfulness.
   - Scripture: "And we know that all things work together for good to them that love God, to them who are the called according to his purpose." (Romans 8:28 KJV)

Reflect on Romans 8:28, which assures us that God works all things for our good when we love Him and follow His purpose. How can this truth reshape our perspective on internal struggles?

2. Seeking God's Perspective
   - Pray for wisdom and discernment to understand God's will amidst internal conflicts. Surrender your doubts and fears to Him in prayer, trusting His plan.
   - Scripture: "Trust in the Lord with all your heart, and do not lean on your understanding. In all your ways acknowledge him, and he will make straight your paths." (Proverbs 3:5-6 KJV)

Proverbs 3:5- 6 encourages us to trust God entirely and seek His guidance in all our lives. How can trusting in God's wisdom help us overcome internal barriers?

Exercise: Overcoming Internal Barriers

1. Self-Reflection
   o Take a moment to reflect on any doubts, fears, or negative thoughts that have held you back from fully embracing God's plan for your life.
   o Write down these internal barriers and identify specific Scriptures that counteract these negative thoughts with God's truth.
2. Prayer and Surrender
   o Spend dedicated time in prayer, surrendering these internal barriers to God. Pour out your heart honestly and ask Him to replace your doubts and fears with His peace and confidence in His perfect plan.
   o Scripture: "Cast all your anxiety on him because he cares for you." (1 Peter 5:7 KJV)
   o Use 1 Peter 5:7 as a guide to relinquish your worries to God, knowing He cares deeply for you and desires to lift your burdens.
3. Seeking Accountability
   o Share your struggles with a trusted friend, mentor, or small group leader who can provide biblical encouragement and pray with you.
   o Scripture: "Therefore, confess your sins to one another and pray for one another, that you may be healed. The prayer of a righteous person has great power as it is working." (James 5:16 KJV)
   o According to James 5:16, opening up to fellow believers and praying together can

bring healing and strength. How can you rely on your Christian community to support you in overcoming internal barriers?

4. Action Steps

   o Identify practical steps you can take to confront and overcome each internal barrier. These steps may include memorizing Scripture, journaling your thoughts and prayers, or seeking professional Christian counseling.

   o Scripture: "For though we walk in the flesh, we do not war after the flesh: For the weapons of our warfare are not carnal, but mighty through God to the pulling down of strongholds." (2 Corinthians 10:3-4 KJV)

   o Reflect on 2 Corinthians 10:3-4, which reminds us that our spiritual battles require God's supernatural strength. How can you actively engage in spiritual warfare to dismantle internal barriers?

Conclusion

In Week 8, we've explored the internal barriers that can hinder us from fulfilling God's purpose for our lives. We can effectively overcome these obstacles by engaging in self-reflection, fervent prayer, seeking accountability, and taking intentional action steps. Remember, God is faithful, and His Word is powerful to transform our minds and hearts. As you continue to pursue God's calling with courage and reliance on His strength, may you experience His abundant grace and guidance every step of the way.

Overall Conclusion

Congratulations on completing the Biblical Life Purpose course! Throughout these weeks, we've embarked on a journey to discover and fulfill God's unique plan for our lives. Let's take a moment to reflect on what we've learned and how we can continue to grow in our faith journey.

Reflecting on Our Journey

1. Understanding God's Word: We've explored the importance of grounding our life's purpose in God's Word, seeking His wisdom and guidance through Scripture.
    o Scripture: "Thy word is a lamp unto my feet and a light unto my path." (Psalm 119:105 KJV)
2. Embracing Jesus' Teachings: By studying Jesus' teachings, we've learned principles of love, forgiveness, and service that shape our purpose and interactions with others.
    o Scripture: "A new commandment I give unto you, That ye love one another; as I have loved you, that ye also love one another. By this shall all men know that ye are my disciples if ye have love one to another." (John 13:34-35 KJV)
3. Empowered by the Holy Spirit: Through the Holy Spirit, we've experienced God's presence, guidance, and empowerment in pursuing His calling.
    o Scripture: "But ye shall receive power, after that the Holy Ghost comes upon you: and ye

shall be witnesses unto me both in Jerusalem, and in all Judaea, and Samaria, and unto the uttermost part of the earth." (Acts 1:8 KJV)

4. Equipped with the Full Armor of God: We've put on the whole armor of God to stand firm against spiritual opposition and to live boldly for Christ.
   o Scripture: "Finally, my brethren, be strong in the Lord, and in the power of his might. Put on the whole armour of God, that ye may be able to stand against the wiles of the devil." (Ephesians 6:10-11 KJV)

5. Encouraged by Brothers and Sisters in Christ: In fellowship with other believers, we've found support, encouragement, and accountability to walk faithfully in our purpose.
   o Scripture: "And let us consider one another to provoke unto love and to good works: Not forsaking the assembling of ourselves together, as the manner of some is; but exhorting one another: and so much the more, as ye see the day approaching." (Hebrews 10:24-25 KJV)

Applying Our Learning

As we conclude, let's consider how we can apply these principles moving forward:

- Living Purposefully: Continually seek God's guidance in all decisions, trusting His plan for our lives.

- Scripture: "Trust in the Lord with all thine heart, and lean not unto thine own understanding. In all thy ways acknowledge him, and he shall direct thy paths." (Proverbs 3:5-6 KJV)
- Serving Others: Use our spiritual gifts and strengths to serve others and share the love of Christ.
  - Scripture: "As every man hath received the gift, even so, minister the same one to another, as good stewards of the manifold grace of God." (1 Peter 4:10 KJV)
- Remaining Faithful: Stay obedient to God's Word, even in the face of challenges, knowing He is faithful to His promises.
  - Scripture: "For ye need patience, that, after ye have done the will of God, ye might receive the promise." (Hebrews 10:36 KJV)

Moving Forward

As we step out in faith, remember that our journey doesn't end here. It's a lifelong pursuit of growing closer to God, discovering His purpose for us, and making an eternal impact. Let's continue to rely on God's strength, seek His will daily, and encourage one another in our walk of faith.

Prayer

Let's close in prayer, thanking God for His guidance throughout this course and asking for His continued presence as we live out our purpose for His glory.

---

May God bless you abundantly as you continue to live out His purpose passionately and passionately. Keep seeking Him, trusting Him, and walking in obedience, knowing He has a beautiful plan for us.

# Biblical Empowerment for Youth Course Manual

## Course Overview

Welcome to the **Biblical Empowerment for Youth** course. This self-paced course is designed for parents, guardians, and trusted adults to guide youth using God's Word, Jesus' teachings, and the Holy Spirit. The course equips you to help children, adolescents, and teens grow spiritually, face challenges, and overcome obstacles. Drawing from the Bible (King James Version), you will learn how to empower youth using the **Full Body of Armor**, God's Angels, Brothers and Sisters in Christ, and various aspects of faith. By the end of this course, you will be equipped to help youth develop resilience, set goals, and live purpose-driven lives.

## Course Objectives

By the end of this course, participants will:
1. Understand the stages of change and assess satisfaction in various life circumstances.
2. Explore how God's love shapes worldviews and influences personal development.
3. Identify and nurture youth's passions, personality traits, strengths, and spiritual gifts.
4. Build community among Brothers and Sisters in Christ for support and spiritual growth.
5. Clarify a vision and faith system for spiritual growth in young people.
6. Develop a mission-driven approach using God's assurance and create effective strategies.

7. Set goals, take actionable steps, and utilize the Full Body of Armor for protection and strength.
8. Overcome external and internal barriers through obedience, faith, and biblical principles.

Weekly Introductions

Week 1: Awareness - The Stages of Change, Satisfaction Assessment, Circumstances,

Worldviews, & God's Love

Introduction: In Week 1, we will focus on understanding the stages of change and how to assess satisfaction in various areas of life. We'll explore how God's love shapes circumstances and worldviews. By the end of this week, you will be equipped to guide youth through these changes with a biblical perspective.

Example to Illustrate Concepts:
- Stages of Change: Discuss how the story of Saul's transformation to Paul (Acts 9) represents the stages of spiritual change.
- Satisfaction Assessment: Use a satisfaction wheel to help youth assess critical areas of life (e.g., spiritual life, relationships, education).
- Worldviews: Explore the differences between Joseph's worldview and his brothers' perspectives (Genesis 37).

———

Week 2: Awareness - Passions, Personality, Strengths, Spiritual Gifts, & Brothers and

Sisters in Christ

Introduction: This week focuses on discovering passions, identifying strengths, understanding personality, and recognizing spiritual gifts in youth. We'll also explore the significance of fellowship with Brothers and Sisters in Christ for spiritual growth.

Example to Illustrate Concepts:
- Passions and Strengths: Reflect on David's passion for music and strength in battle (1 Samuel 16-17).
- Spiritual Gifts: Examine 1 Corinthians 12 to identify the spiritual gifts youth may possess.
- Brothers and Sisters in Christ: Highlight how the early Church community supported each other (Acts 2:42-47).

Week 3: Vision - Clarify the Vision & The Faith System

Introduction: In Week 3, we focus on clarifying the vision for youth's spiritual and personal growth and deepening their faith system. By guiding youth to articulate their vision, you help them develop clarity in their spiritual journey.

Example to Illustrate Concepts:
- Clarifying Vision: Study Moses' encounter at the burning bush (Exodus 3) as an example of vision clarification.
- Faith System: Discuss Abraham's faith journey, particularly how his trust in God shaped his life decisions (Genesis 12:1-9).

Week 4: Vision - Moving with the Mission & God's Assurance

Introduction: Week 4 is about moving forward with a clear mission grounded in God's assurance. You will guide youth in aligning their actions with their mission while relying on God's promises for strength and direction.

Example to Illustrate Concepts:
- Mission Statements: Help youth create a personal mission statement using Nehemiah's response to rebuilding Jerusalem (Nehemiah 1-2).
- God's Assurance: Explore the assurance God gave to Joshua before leading Israel into the Promised Land (Joshua 1:1-9).

Week 5: Strategy and Action - Create a Strategy & Strength

Introduction: This week focuses on creating strategies for spiritual growth, using personal strengths, and relying on God's power. By the end of this week, you will be equipped with tools to help youth implement their spiritual development plan.

Example to Illustrate Concepts:
- Strategy Creation: Study how Joshua strategized to conquer Jericho (Joshua 6).
- Entire Body of Armor: Examine Ephesians 6:11-18, guiding youth to role-play how to use each piece of the armor in spiritual warfare.

Week 6: Strategy and Action - Setting Goals, Taking Action, Moving the Process Forward & The Full Body of Armor

Introduction: In Week 6, we focus on goal-setting, taking actionable steps, and continuing the process of spiritual growth. We'll also explore the role of the Full Body of Armor in spiritual battles.

Example to Illustrate Concepts:
- Setting Goals: Study Paul's missionary journeys to see how setting goals led to spreading the Gospel (Acts 13-21).
- Taking Action: Reflect on Ruth's proactive steps to provide for herself and Naomi (Ruth 2).
- The Full Body of Armor: Guide youth in using the Shield of Faith to counter doubts and fears (Ephesians 6:16).

Week 7: Obstacles - External Barriers, Energy Drainers & Obedience

Introduction: Week 7 addresses how to overcome external barriers and energy drainers. We will also discuss the importance of obedience in maintaining focus and spiritual strength.

Example to Illustrate Concepts:

- External Barriers: Explore Nehemiah's challenges while rebuilding the wall (Nehemiah 4).
- Energy Drainers: Study Elijah's experience of exhaustion and renewal by God (1 Kings 19).
- Obedience: Reflect on Jonah's disobedience and its consequences (Book of Jonah).

---

Week 8: Obstacles - Internal Barriers and Getting Past the Barriers

Introduction: In the final week, we will focus on identifying and overcoming internal barriers that hinder spiritual growth. Helping youth navigate these obstacles will lead to resilience and deeper faith.

Example to Illustrate Concepts:
- Internal Barriers: Discuss Peter's struggle with fear as he walked on water (Matthew 14:28-31).
- Overcoming Barriers: Study Gideon's transformation from fear to leadership (Judges 6-7).
- Resilience: Reflect on Paul's words about strength in weakness through God's grace (2 Corinthians 12:9-10).

---

Biblical Example of Empowerment: The Story of David

1. Name: David
2. Story Overview: From shepherd to king, David's journey shows how faith and obedience empower individuals.
3. Experiences: David's anointing, victory over Goliath, and rise to kingship showcase trust in God.
4. Spiritual Connection: His prayers and psalms (e.g., Psalm 23) demonstrate his reliance on God's protection.
5. Overcoming Barriers: David faced opposition, jealousy, and personal failures but remained faithful.
6. The Role of the Devil: The devil tried to derail David through various challenges, but David's faith prevailed.
7. Combating Through Prayer and Scriptures: David's prayers (e.g., Psalm 51) show repentance and reliance on God's mercy.

———

Conclusion

This course provides a comprehensive guide to empowering youth through biblical principles. As you move forward, reflect on how God equips each young person with unique strengths and spiritual gifts, and remain steadfast in guiding them with faith and love.

**Biblical Empowerment for Youth**

Welcome to the Biblical Empowerment course for parents, guardians, and trusted adults. This self-paced course will guide you using God's Word, Jesus' teachings, and the Holy Spirit to help children, adolescents, and teens grow spiritually and face life's challenges. You will learn how to empower the youth through the Full Body of Armor, God's Angels, the support of Brothers and Sisters in Christ, and various aspects of faith and belief systems. The course also explores stages of change, God's love, and practical examples tailored for different age groups. Using the Bible's King James Version (KJV), you will gain insights and tools to foster spiritual growth and resilience in young people.

## Course Objectives

1. Understand the stages of change and assess satisfaction in various life circumstances.
2. Explore God's love and its implications on worldview and personal development.
3. Identify and nurture passions, personality traits, strengths, spiritual gifts, and belief systems.
4. Foster a sense of community among Brothers and Sisters in Christ.
5. Clarify personal vision and faith system for spiritual growth.
6. Develop a mission-driven approach with God's assurance and create effective strategies.
7. Set goals, take actionable steps, and use the Full Body of Armor for protection and strength.

8. Overcome external and internal obstacles through obedience, faith, and biblical principles.

Week 1: Awareness - The Stages of Change, Satisfaction Assessment, Circumstances, World Views & God's Love

Introduction

In this first week, we will focus on understanding the stages of change and assessing satisfaction in various aspects of life. We will explore how God's love influences circumstances and worldviews. By the end of this week, you will have a foundational understanding of how to guide youth through changes with a biblical perspective.

Week 2: Awareness - Passions, Personality, Strengths, Spiritual Gifts, Belief System, & Brothers and Sisters In Christ

Introduction

Week 2 delves into discovering and nurturing passions, personality traits, strengths, and spiritual gifts in youth. We will also examine the importance of belief systems and the support network of Brothers and Sisters in Christ. This week aims to help you identify and cultivate the unique qualities God has placed in the young people you are guiding.

Week 3: Vision - Clarify the Vision & The Faith System

Introduction

This week is about clarifying the vision and understanding the faith system. We will discuss how to help youth develop a clear vision for their spiritual and personal lives grounded in faith. You will learn techniques to strengthen their faith system and guide their spiritual journey.

## Week 4: Vision - Moving with the Mission & God's Assurance

Introduction

In Week 4, we will focus on moving forward with God's mission on the youth's hearts, emphasizing God's assurance. You will learn how to guide young people in aligning their actions with their mission and relying on God's promises for assurance and confidence.

## Week 5: Strategy and Action - Create a Strategy & Strength

Introduction

This week, we will discuss creating a spiritual growth and personal development strategy. We will explore harnessing God's strength to implement this strategy effectively. By the end of this week, you will be equipped with practical tools to help youth plan and execute their spiritual goals.

## Week 6: Strategy and Action - Setting Goals, Taking Action, Moving the Process Forward & The Full Body of Armor

Introduction

Week 6 is about setting specific goals, taking actionable steps, and moving the process forward. We will also cover the importance of the Full Body of Armor as described in

Ephesians 6:11-18 and how to use it to protect and strengthen youth in their spiritual journey.

Week 7: Obstacles - External Barriers, Energy Drainers & Obedience

Introduction

This week focuses on identifying and overcoming external barriers and energy drainers. We will discuss the role of obedience to God in overcoming these obstacles. You will learn strategies to help youth navigate challenges from outside influences and maintain their spiritual vitality.

Week 8: Obstacles - Internal Barriers and Getting Past the Barriers

Introduction

In the final week, we will address internal barriers that hinder spiritual growth. We will explore methods to help youth overcome these internal obstacles through faith and biblical principles. By the end of this week, you will have a comprehensive understanding of how to guide youth past their internal struggles and toward a closer relationship with God.

Biblical Example of Empowerment: The Story of David

1. Name: David

2. Story Overview

David, the shepherd boy who became king, is a prime example of biblical empowerment. His journey from tending sheep to leading Israel demonstrates the power of faith, obedience, and reliance on God.

3. Experiences

David's experiences include his anointing by Samuel, his victory over Goliath, his years fleeing King Saul, and his ultimate ascension to the throne. Throughout these experiences, David demonstrated trust in God and perseverance.

4. Spiritual Connection and Overcoming Barriers

David's connection with God was evident in his psalms and prayers. He overcame barriers such as fear, opposition, and personal failures by seeking God's guidance and strength. Psalm 23 is a testament to his reliance on God's protection and provision.

6. The Role of the Devil

The devil sought to derail David through various means, including jealousy from Saul, personal sin, and rebellion within his family. Despite these attacks, David remained steadfast in his faith.

7. Combating Through Prayer and Scriptures (KJV Only)

Like those in Psalm 51, David's prayers show his repentance and reliance on God's mercy. Scriptures such as Psalm 27:1 ("The Lord is my light and my salvation; whom shall I fear?") illustrate his trust in God's protection and deliverance.

Conclusion

This course on Biblical Empowerment for Youth provides a comprehensive framework for guiding young people through spiritual and personal growth using biblical principles. By understanding the stages of change, nurturing individual strengths and spiritual gifts, clarifying vision and mission, creating strategies, and overcoming obstacles, you can empower the youth to develop a robust and resilient faith. The story of David serves as a powerful example of how to live a life empowered by God, overcoming challenges through faith, prayer, and reliance on the Scriptures. May this course equip you to lead and inspire the next generation in their walk with God.

Week 1: Awareness - The Stages of Change, Satisfaction Assessment, Circumstances, World Views & God's Love

Introduction

Welcome to Week 1 of our course on Biblical Empowerment for Youth. This week, we will focus on building awareness, starting with understanding the stages of change, assessing satisfaction in various aspects of life, examining circumstances and worldviews, and, most importantly, exploring God's love. By the end of this week, you will have a foundational understanding of how to guide youth through changes with a biblical perspective.

The Stages of Change

Understanding the stages of change is essential in helping youth navigate their spiritual and personal development. The stages of change include:

1. Pre-contemplation: At this stage, individuals still need to be made aware of the need for change.
2. Contemplation: Here, individuals begin to recognize the need for change and start considering it.
3. Preparation: In this stage, individuals plan and prepare for the change.
4. Action: This stage involves actively making changes and implementing new behaviors.
5. Maintenance: Individuals work to sustain the changes they have made.

Biblical Perspective

- Ecclesiastes 3:1 (KJV): "To everything there is a season, and a time to every purpose under the heaven."
- Romans 12:2 (KJV): "And be not conformed to this world: but be ye transformed by the renewing of your mind, that ye may prove what is that good, and acceptable, and perfect, will of God."

Satisfaction Assessment

Assessing satisfaction in various aspects of life helps identify areas that need attention and improvement. Encourage youth to reflect on their satisfaction in spiritual life, relationships, academics, and personal goals.

Exercise

1. Reflective Journaling: Have the youth write down their thoughts on different areas of their life. Ask them to rate their satisfaction on a scale of 1-10.
2. Discussion: Discuss why they rated each area as they did and what changes they feel could improve their satisfaction.

Biblical Perspective

- Psalm 139:23-24 (KJV): "Search me, O God, and know my heart: try me, and know my thoughts: And see if there be any wicked way in me, and lead me in the way everlasting."

Circumstances and Worldviews

Understanding how circumstances and worldviews affect behavior and decisions is crucial in guiding youth. Help them see how their environment and culture influence their thoughts and actions.

Exercise

1.  Case Studies: Present various scenarios that youth might encounter and discuss how they could respond from a biblical perspective.
2.  Role-Playing: Have youth act out different situations to explore how they might react and make decisions based on their faith.

Biblical Perspective

- Romans 12:2 (KJV): "And be not conformed to this world: but be ye transformed by the renewing of your mind, that ye may prove what is that good, and acceptable, and perfect, will of God."
- Colossians 3:2 (KJV): "Set your affection on things above, not on things on the earth."

God's Love

God's love is the foundation of our faith and the driving force behind actual change and satisfaction. Understanding and experiencing God's love can transform lives.

Key Points

1. Unconditional Love: God's love is not based on our performance but His nature.
2. Transformative Power: God's love can change hearts and minds.
3. Security and Assurance: Knowing God's love provides security and assurance in all circumstances.

Exercise

1. Bible Study: Read and reflect on passages that speak of God's love, such as John 3:16, Romans 8:38-39, and 1 John 4:9-10.
2. Prayer: Encourage youth to pray, asking God to help them understand and feel His love more deeply.

Biblical Perspective

- John 3:16 (KJV): "For God so loved the world, that he gave his only begotten Son, that whosoever believeth in him should not perish, but have everlasting life."
- Romans 8:38-39 (KJV): "For I am persuaded, that neither death, nor life, nor angels, nor principalities, nor powers, nor things present, nor things to come, Nor height, nor depth, nor any other creature, shall be able to separate us from the love of God, which is in Christ Jesus our Lord."
- 1 John 4:9-10 (KJV): "In this was manifested the love of God toward us, because that God sent his

only begotten Son into the world, that we might live through him. Herein is love, not that we loved God, but that he loved us and sent his Son to be the propitiation for our sins."

Conclusion

This week, you have been introduced to the foundational concepts of change, satisfaction, circumstances, worldviews, and God's love. As you continue through this course, keep these principles in mind and apply them as you guide the youth in your life. Next week, we will explore passions, personality, strengths, spiritual gifts, belief systems, and the importance of Brothers and Sisters in Christ.

Week 2: Awareness - Passions, Personality, Strengths, Spiritual Gifts, Belief System, & Brothers and Sisters In Christ

Introduction

Welcome to Week 2 of our course on Biblical Empowerment for Youth. This week, we will focus on helping youth understand and develop their passions, personalities, strengths, spiritual gifts, belief systems, and the importance of community among Brothers and Sisters in Christ. By the end of this week, you will be equipped to help the youth identify and cultivate the unique qualities and support networks that God has placed in their lives.

## Passions

Helping youth discover their passions is vital for their personal and spiritual growth. Passions are the activities, subjects, or causes that inspire and energize them.

## Exercise

1. Interest Inventory: Have the youth list activities, hobbies, and subjects they are passionate about.
2. Discussion: Discuss how these passions can be aligned with God's purpose for their lives.

## Biblical Perspective

- Colossians 3:23 (KJV): "And whatsoever ye do, do it heartily, as to the Lord, and not unto men."
- Psalm 37:4 (KJV): "Delight thyself also in the Lord, and he shall give thee the desires of thine heart."

## Personality

Understanding personality helps youth recognize their inherent traits and how they interact with others. It includes introversion/extroversion, thinking/feeling, and sensing/intuition.

## Exercise

1. Personality Assessment: Use a simple personality test or a discussion-based method to help youth identify their personality traits.

2. Reflection: Reflect on how these traits influence their relationships and activities.

Biblical Perspective

- Psalm 139:14 (KJV): "I will praise thee; for I am fearfully and wonderfully made: marvelous are thy works; and that my soul knoweth right well."

Strengths

Recognizing and developing strengths enables youth to use their God-given abilities effectively.

Exercise

1. Strengths Identification: Have the youth list their strengths and provide examples of how they have used them.
2. Encouragement: Encourage them to seek opportunities to use their strengths to serve others and God.

Biblical Perspective

- Philippians 4:13 (KJV): "I can do all things through Christ which strengtheneth me."
- 1 Peter 4:10 (KJV): "As every man hath received the gift, even so, minister the same one to another, as good stewards of the manifold grace of God."

Spiritual Gifts

Spiritual gifts are special abilities given by the Holy Spirit to believers to build up the body of Christ.

Exercise

1. Spiritual Gifts Inventory: Provide a spiritual gifts assessment or facilitate a discussion to help youth identify their spiritual gifts.
2. Application: Discuss ways to use their spiritual gifts in church and community.

Biblical Perspective

- 1 Corinthians 12:4-7 (KJV): "Now there are diversities of gifts, but the same Spirit. There are differences in administrations, but they have the same Lord. And there are diversities of operations, but the same God works all in all. But the manifestation of the Spirit is given to every man to profit withal."

Belief System

A robust belief system grounded in biblical truth is essential for spiritual growth and resilience.

Exercise

1. Statement of Faith: Have the youth write a personal statement outlining their core beliefs.

2. Discussion: Discuss the importance of these beliefs and how they influence daily decisions and actions.

Biblical Perspective

- 2 Timothy 3:16-17 (KJV): "All scripture is given by inspiration of God, and is profitable for doctrine, for reproof, for correction, for instruction in righteousness: That the man of God may be perfect, thoroughly furnished unto all good works."
- Hebrews 11:1 (KJV): "Now faith is the substance of things hoped for, the evidence of things not seen."

Brothers and Sisters In Christ

The community of believers plays a crucial role in supporting and encouraging each other in faith.

Exercise

1. Community Building: Encourage youth to participate in church activities and small groups to build relationships with other believers.
2. Service Projects: Organize service projects where youth can work together to serve others and strengthen their bonds.

Biblical Perspective

- Hebrews 10:24-25 (KJV): "And let us consider one another to provoke unto love and to good works: Not forsaking the assembling of ourselves together, as the manner of some is; but exhorting one another: and so much the more, as ye see the day approaching."

- Galatians 6:2 (KJV): "Bear ye one another's burdens, and so fulfill the law of Christ."

Conclusion

This week, you have explored the importance of passions, personality, strengths, spiritual gifts, belief systems, and community among Brothers and Sisters in Christ. These elements are critical for the personal and spiritual development of youth. As you guide them, remember to encourage their unique qualities and foster solid and supportive relationships within the Christian community.

Next week, we will focus on clarifying vision and understanding the faith system to further guide the youth in their spiritual journey.

Week 3: Vision - Clarify the Vision & The Faith System

Introduction

Welcome to Week 3 of our course on Biblical Empowerment for Youth. This week, we will focus on helping youth clarify their vision for their lives and understand the importance of a robust faith system. By the end of this week, you will be equipped to guide youth in developing a clear vision grounded in faith, providing them with direction and purpose in their spiritual journey.

Clarify the Vision

A clear vision is essential for guiding youth towards their God-given purpose. Vision provides direction, motivation, and a sense of purpose.

Steps to Clarify Vision

1. Seek God's Guidance
   - Encourage youth to pray and seek God's guidance in discovering their vision.
   - Scripture: "Trust in the Lord with all thine heart, and lean not unto thine own understanding. In all thy ways acknowledge him, and he shall direct thy paths." (Proverbs 3:5-6 KJV)
2. Identify Passions and Talents
   - Help youth identify their passions and talents, often aligning with God's purpose.
   - Scripture: "For I know the thoughts that I think toward you, saith the Lord, thoughts of peace, and not of evil, to give you an expected end." (Jeremiah 29:11 KJV)
3. Set Long-term Goals
   - Guide youth in setting long-term goals that reflect their vision and align with their faith.
   - Scripture: "Where there is no vision, the people perish: but he that keepeth the law, happy is he." (Proverbs 29:18 KJV)
4. Create a Vision Statement
   - Help youth write a personal vision statement that articulates their goals and aspirations.

- Scripture: "I press toward the mark for the prize of the high calling of God in Christ Jesus." (Philippians 3:14 KJV)

Exercise

1. Vision Board: Have the youth create a vision board with images, words, and scriptures representing their vision.
2. Reflection: Facilitate a reflection session where youth can share their vision boards and discuss their aspirations.

The Faith System

A robust faith system provides the foundation for achieving and sustaining a clear vision. It involves trusting in God, understanding His Word, and living according to biblical principles.

Components of a Strong Faith System

1. Trust in God
   - Encourage youth to place their trust in God in all circumstances.
   - Scripture: "But without faith, it is impossible to please him: for he that cometh to God must believe that he is and that he is a rewarder of them that diligently seek him." (Hebrews 11:6 KJV)
2. Knowledge of God's Word
   - Emphasize the importance of studying and understanding the Bible.

- Scripture: "Study to shew thyself approved unto God, a workman that needeth not to be ashamed, rightly dividing the word of truth." (2 Timothy 2:15 KJV)

3. Prayer and Communion with God
   - Teach youth the importance of regular prayer and communion with God.
   - Scripture: "Pray without ceasing." (1 Thessalonians 5:17 KJV)
4. Living by Faith
   - Encourage youth to live by faith and not by sight, trusting God's plan for their lives.
   - Scripture: "For we walk by faith, not by sight." (2 Corinthians 5:7 KJV)

Exercise

1. Faith Journal: Have the youth keep a journal to record their prayers, scriptures, and reflections on their spiritual journey.
2. Bible Study Group: Organize a Bible study group focused on understanding faith and how to apply it in daily life.

Application of Vision and Faith

1. Setting Short-term Goals
   - Guide youth in setting short-term goals aligned with their vision and faith.
   - Scripture: "Commit thy works unto the Lord, and thy thoughts shall be established." (Proverbs 16:3 KJV)
2. Accountability Partners

- o Encourage youth to find accountability partners to support and encourage them in their spiritual journey.
- o Scripture: "Iron sharpeneth iron; so a man sharpeneth the countenance of his friend." (Proverbs 27:17 KJV)

Conclusion

This week, you have learned how to help youth clarify their vision and strengthen their faith. By guiding them in these areas, you give them the direction and foundation needed for their spiritual and personal growth. As they develop a clear vision grounded in faith, they will be better equipped to pursue their God-given purpose with confidence and resilience.

Next week, we will focus on moving with the mission, understanding God's assurance, helping youth align their actions with their mission, and trusting God's promises.

Week 4: Vision - Moving with the Mission & God's Assurance

Introduction

Welcome to Week 4 of our course on Biblical Empowerment for Youth. This week, we will focus on moving forward with the mission that God has placed on the youth's hearts, emphasizing the importance of God's assurance. By the end of this week, you will be equipped to help youth align their actions with their mission and rely on God's promises for assurance and confidence.

Moving with the Mission

Once a clear vision is established, taking actionable steps to move forward with the mission is essential. This involves setting concrete goals, making plans, and taking steps in faith.

Steps to Move with the Mission

1. Set Specific Goals
   o Help youth set specific, measurable, attainable, relevant, and time-bound (SMART) goals that align with their vision.
   o Scripture: "Commit thy works unto the Lord, and thy thoughts shall be established." (Proverbs 16:3 KJV)
2. Create an Action Plan
   o Guide youth to create a detailed action plan outlining the steps needed to achieve their goals.
   o Scripture: "For which of you, intending to build a tower, sitteth not down first, and counteth the cost, whether he have sufficient to finish it?" (Luke 14:28 KJV)
3. Take Action in Faith
   o Encourage youth to take steps of faith, trusting that God will guide and provide for them.
   o Scripture: "Now faith is the substance of things hoped for, the evidence of things not seen." (Hebrews 11:1 KJV)
4. Stay Committed

- Teach youth the importance of staying committed to their mission, even when facing challenges.
- Scripture: "And let us not be weary in well doing: for in due season we shall reap if we faint not." (Galatians 6:9 KJV)

Exercise

1. Goal-Setting Workshop: Conduct a workshop where youth can set specific goals for their mission and create action plans.
2. Progress Tracking: Have youth track their progress and reflect on their experiences and adjustments needed.

God's Assurance

God's assurance provides the confidence and security needed to pursue one's mission with faith and resilience. It is rooted in His promises and faithfulness.

Critical Aspects of God's Assurance

1. God's Promises
   - Teach youth about the promises of God that assure their journey.
   - Scripture: "For all the promises of God in him are yea, and in him Amen, unto the glory of God by us." (2 Corinthians 1:20 KJV)
2. God's Presence

- Emphasize that God is always with them, providing guidance and comfort.
- Scripture: "Fear thou not; for I am with thee: be not dismayed; for I am thy God: I will strengthen thee; yea, I will help thee; yea, I will uphold thee with the right hand of my righteousness." (Isaiah 41:10 KJV)

3. God's Provision
   - Encourage youth to trust that God will provide for their needs as they pursue their mission.
   - Scripture: "But my God shall supply all your need according to his riches in glory by Christ Jesus." (Philippians 4:19 KJV)

4. God's Faithfulness
   - Remind youth that God is faithful and will fulfill His promises.
   - Scripture: "Let us hold fast the profession of our faith without wavering; (for he is faithful that promised;)" (Hebrews 10:23 KJV)

Exercise

1. Scripture Memorization: Have youth memorize key scriptures emphasizing God's promises and assurance.
2. Faith Stories: Encourage youth to share personal stories or testimonies where they have experienced God's assurance and faithfulness.

Application of Mission and Assurance

1. Daily Devotionals
   - ○ Encourage youth to start each day with a devotional time to seek God's guidance and assurance.
   - ○ Scripture: "Thy word is a lamp unto my feet and a light unto my path." (Psalm 119:105 KJV)
2. Prayer Partners
   - ○ Pair youth with prayer partners to support each other in their mission and pray for God's assurance.
   - ○ Scripture: "Again I say unto you, That if two of you shall agree on earth as touching anything that they shall ask, it shall be done for them of my Father which is in heaven." (Matthew 18:19 KJV)
3. Service Opportunities
   - ○ Provide opportunities for youth to serve others as part of their mission, reinforcing the application of their vision in real-world contexts.
   - ○ Scripture: "For even the Son of man came not to be ministered unto, but to minister, and to give his life a ransom for many." (Mark 10:45 KJV)

Conclusion

This week, you have learned how to help youth continue their mission and rely on God's assurance. By guiding them in setting goals, creating action plans, and trusting in God's promises, you give them the tools and confidence to pursue their God-given purpose. As they continue their spiritual journey, remind them that God is always with them, providing guidance, provision, and assurance.

Next week, we will focus on creating a strategy and harnessing strength, equipping youth with practical tools and spiritual resilience to achieve their goals.

Week 5: Strategy and Action - Create a Strategy & Strength

Introduction

Welcome to Week 5 of our course on Biblical Empowerment for Youth. This week, we will focus on creating a practical strategy to achieve the vision and mission that youth have developed. Additionally, we will explore the concept of strength from a biblical perspective, emphasizing the importance of relying on God's strength in all endeavors. By the end of this week, you will be equipped to help youth develop actionable plans and draw on spiritual strength to carry out their mission.

Create a Strategy

Creating a strategy involves developing a clear plan of action that outlines the steps needed to achieve specific goals. A well-thought-out strategy provides direction, clarity, and motivation.

Steps to Create a Strategy

1. Define Objectives

- o Help youth define clear and specific objectives that align with their vision and mission.
- o Scripture: "The plans of the diligent lead surely to plenty, but those of everyone who is hasty, surely to poverty." (Proverbs 21:5 KJV)

2. Identify Resources
   - o Identify the resources (time, skills, materials) needed to achieve the objectives.
   - o Scripture: "But my God shall supply all your need according to his riches in glory by Christ Jesus." (Philippians 4:19 KJV)

3. Develop a Timeline
   - o Create a timeline that outlines when each plan step should be completed.
   - o Scripture: "To everything there is a season, and a time to every purpose under the heaven." (Ecclesiastes 3:1 KJV)

4. Assign Responsibilities
   - o Determine who is responsible for each part of the plan, encouraging collaboration and accountability.
   - o Scripture: "Two are better than one; because they have a good reward for their labor." (Ecclesiastes 4:9 KJV)

5. Monitor Progress
   - o Establish a method for tracking progress and making necessary adjustments.
   - o Scripture: "Examine yourselves, whether ye be in the faith; prove your selves. Know ye, not your selves, how that Jesus Christ is in

you, except ye be reprobates?" (2
Corinthians 13:5 KJV)

Exercise

1. Strategy Planning Session: Conduct a planning
   session where youth can work on creating detailed
   strategies for their goals.
2. Strategy Map: Have youth create a visual strategy
   map that outlines their objectives, resources,
   timeline, and responsibilities.

Strength

Understanding and harnessing strength from a biblical
perspective involves recognizing that true strength comes
from God. It is about relying on His power and grace to
overcome challenges and achieve goals.

Critical Aspects of Biblical Strength

1. God as the Source of Strength
   ○ Emphasize that God is the ultimate source of
     strength and that we should rely on Him.
   ○ Scripture: "I can do all things through Christ
     which strengtheneth me." (Philippians 4:13
     KJV)
2. Strength in Weakness
   ○ Teach that God's strength is made perfect in
     our weakness, encouraging humility and
     dependence on Him.
   ○ Scripture: "And he said unto me, My grace
     is sufficient for thee: for my strength is

perfect in weakness. Therefore, I will most gladly glory in my infirmities, that the power of Christ may rest upon me." (2 Corinthians 12:9 KJV)

3. Courage and Boldness
   o Encourage youth to be courageous and bold, knowing God is with them.
   o Scripture: "Have not I commanded thee? Be strong and of a good courage; be not afraid, neither be thou dismayed: for the Lord thy God is with thee whithersoever thou goest." (Joshua 1:9 KJV)

4. Strength through the Holy Spirit
   o Highlight the role of the Holy Spirit in empowering and strengthening believers.
   o Scripture: "But ye shall receive power, after that the Holy Ghost comes upon you: and ye shall be witnesses unto me both in Jerusalem, and in all Judaea, and Samaria, and unto the uttermost part of the earth." (Acts 1:8 KJV)

Exercise

1. Strength Reflection: Have youth reflect on times when they felt weak and how God provided strength. Please encourage them to journal these experiences.
2. Scripture Study: Organize a study session focused on scriptures emphasizing God's strength and power in our lives.

Application of Strategy and Strength

1. Implementing the Strategy
   - Guide youth in taking the first steps to implement their strategy, reminding them to rely on God's strength throughout the process.
   - Scripture: "Commit thy way unto the Lord; trust also in him; and he shall bring it to pass." (Psalm 37:5 KJV)
2. Strength in Action
   - Encourage youth to take action confidently, knowing God's strength is available.
   - Scripture: "The Lord is my strength and my shield; my heart trusted in him, and I am helped: therefore my heart greatly rejoiceth; and with my song will I praise him." (Psalm 28:7 KJV)
3. Regular Check-ins
   - Establish regular check-ins to review progress, celebrate successes, and address challenges.
   - Scripture: "Let us consider one another to provoke unto love and to good works." (Hebrews 10:24 KJV)

Conclusion

This week, you have learned how to help youth create a practical strategy to achieve their vision and mission and understand the importance of relying on God's strength. By guiding them in these areas, you give them the tools and confidence to pursue their goals with faith and resilience.

Next week, we will focus on setting goals, taking action, moving the process forward, and understanding the Full Body of Armor, equipping youth with the spiritual tools needed to navigate challenges and remain steadfast in their journey.

# Week 6: Strategy and Action - Setting Goals, Taking Action, Moving the Process Forward & The Full Body of Armor

## Introduction

Welcome to Week 6 of our course on Biblical Empowerment for Youth. This week, we will focus on setting specific goals, taking action to achieve those goals, and moving the process forward. Additionally, we will explore the concept of the Full Body of Armor as described in Ephesians 6, understanding how it provides spiritual protection and strength. By the end of this week, you will be equipped to help youth set actionable goals, take decisive steps, and rely on the Full Body of Armor to overcome spiritual challenges.

## Setting Goals

Setting clear and achievable goals is essential for progressing towards one's vision and mission. Goals provide direction, motivation, and a sense of purpose.

## Steps to Setting Effective Goals

1. Specificity
   - Ensure that goals are specific and clearly defined.
   - Scripture: "Write the vision, and make it plain upon tables, that he may run that readeth it." (Habakkuk 2:2 KJV)
2. Measurability

- o Goals should be measurable so that progress can be tracked.
- o Scripture: "So teach us to number our days, that we may apply our hearts unto wisdom." (Psalm 90:12 KJV)

3. Achievability
   - o Set goals that are realistic and attainable.
   - o Scripture: "For which of you, intending to build a tower, sitteth not down first, and counteth the cost, whether he have sufficient to finish it?" (Luke 14:28 KJV)

4. Relevance
   - o Goals should align with the youth's vision and God's purpose for their life.
   - o Scripture: "For I know the thoughts that I think toward you, saith the Lord, thoughts of peace, and not of evil, to give you an expected end." (Jeremiah 29:11 KJV)

5. Time-bound
   - o Establish a timeline for achieving goals to maintain focus and urgency.
   - o Scripture: "To everything there is a season, and a time to every purpose under the heaven." (Ecclesiastes 3:1 KJV)

Exercise

1. SMART Goals Workshop: Conduct a workshop where youth can set SMART goals (Specific, Measurable, Achievable, Relevant, and Time-bound).
2. Goal Mapping: Have youth create a map outlining their goals and the steps needed to achieve them.

Taking Action

Taking action involves putting plans into motion and consistently achieving goals. It requires discipline, perseverance, and reliance on God's guidance.

Steps to Taking Effective Action

1. Start with Prayer
   - Begin each action step with prayer, seeking God's guidance and strength.
   - Scripture: "Commit thy way unto the Lord; trust also in him; and he shall bring it to pass." (Psalm 37:5 KJV)
2. Break Down Tasks
   - Break down goals into smaller, manageable tasks.
   - Scripture: "A man's heart deviseth his way: but the Lord directeth his steps." (Proverbs 16:9 KJV)
3. Stay Focused and Disciplined
   - Maintain focus and discipline when working towards goals.
   - Scripture: "He that is faithful in that which is least is faithful also in much: and he that is unjust in the least is unjust also in much." (Luke 16:10 KJV)
4. Seek Support
   - Encourage youth to seek support and accountability from mentors, peers, and family.

- Scripture: "Iron sharpeneth iron; so a man sharpeneth the countenance of his friend." (Proverbs 27:17 KJV)

## Exercise

1. Action Plan Development: Have youth develop detailed action plans for their goals, breaking them into daily or weekly tasks.
2. Accountability Groups: Form small accountability groups where youth can share their goals and progress, providing mutual support and encouragement.

## Moving the Process Forward

Progress requires consistent effort and the ability to overcome obstacles. Encourage youth to stay committed and make adjustments as needed.

## Strategies for Moving Forward

1. Regular Review and Reflection
   - Regularly review goals and reflect on progress, making necessary adjustments.
   - Scripture: "Examine yourselves, whether ye be in the faith; prove your selves. Know ye, not your selves, how that Jesus Christ is in you, except ye be reprobates?" (2 Corinthians 13:5 KJV)
2. Celebrate Milestones
   - Celebrate achievements and milestones to maintain motivation.

- Scripture: "Rejoice evermore." (1 Thessalonians 5:16 KJV)
3. Persevere through Challenges
   - Encourage perseverance and resilience in the face of challenges.
   - Scripture: "And let us not be weary in well doing: for in due season we shall reap if we faint not." (Galatians 6:9 KJV)

Exercise

1. Progress Journals: Have youth keep journals to track their progress, reflect on their experiences, and record lessons learned.
2. Celebration Event: Organize an event to celebrate the achievements and milestones of the youth, reinforcing the importance of perseverance and progress.

The Full Body of Armor

Understanding the Full Body of Armor, as described in Ephesians 6, equips youth with the spiritual tools needed to stand firm against spiritual challenges and temptations.

Components of the Full Body of Armor

1. Belt of Truth
   - Emphasize the importance of living truthfully and standing by the truth of God's Word.

- o Scripture: "Stand, therefore, having your loins girt about with truth." (Ephesians 6:14 KJV)
2. Breastplate of Righteousness
   - o Encourage living a righteous life through faith in Christ.
   - o Scripture: "And having on the breastplate of righteousness." (Ephesians 6:14 KJV)
3. Feet Shod with the Preparation of the Gospel of Peace
   - o Promote readiness to share the gospel and live in peace.
   - o Scripture: "And your feet shod with the preparation of the gospel of peace." (Ephesians 6:15 KJV)
4. Shield of Faith
   - o Teach the importance of faith in deflecting the enemy's attacks.
   - o Scripture: "Above all, taking the shield of faith, wherewith ye shall be able to quench all the fiery darts of the wicked." (Ephesians 6:16 KJV)
5. Helmet of Salvation
   - o Reinforce the assurance of salvation and protection of the mind.
   - o Scripture: "And take the helmet of salvation." (Ephesians 6:17 KJV)
6. Sword of the Spirit
   - o Emphasize the power of God's Word in spiritual battles.
   - o Scripture: "And the sword of the Spirit, which is the word of God." (Ephesians 6:17 KJV)

7. Prayer
   - Highlight the necessity of prayer in maintaining spiritual strength and communication with God.
   - Scripture: "Praying always with all prayer and supplication in the Spirit, and watching thereunto with all perseverance and supplication for all saints." (Ephesians 6:18 KJV)

Exercise

1. Armor Illustration: Have the youth create illustrations or diagrams of the Full Body of Armor, labeling each part and its significance.
2. Role-Playing Scenarios: Conduct role-playing scenarios where youth can practice using the Full Body of Armor in various situations.

Conclusion

This week, you have learned how to help youth set actionable goals, take decisive steps, and rely on the Full Body of Armor for spiritual protection and strength. By guiding them in these areas, you provide them with the practical tools and spiritual resilience to achieve their goals and overcome challenges.

Next week, we will focus on identifying and overcoming external and internal obstacles, equipping youth with strategies to navigate barriers and stay on course in their spiritual and personal journey.

Week 7: Obstacles - External Barriers, Energy Drainers & Obedience

Introduction

Welcome to Week 7 of our course on Biblical Empowerment for Youth. This week, we will focus on identifying and overcoming external barriers and energy drainers that can hinder progress. We will also emphasize the importance of obedience to God's Word as a crucial element in navigating obstacles. By the end of this week, you will be equipped to help youth recognize these challenges and respond to them with spiritual wisdom and practical strategies.

External Barriers

External barriers are obstacles that come from outside circumstances and can impede progress. These can include societal pressures, negative influences, and environmental factors.

Identifying External Barriers

1. Societal Pressures
   o Understand how societal expectations and peer pressure can impact youth.
   o Scripture: "And be not conformed to this world: but be ye transformed by the renewing of your mind, that ye may prove what is that good, and acceptable, and perfect, will of God." (Romans 12:2 KJV)
2. Negative Influences

- Identify negative influences, such as unhealthy friendships or media content.
- Scripture: "Be not deceived: evil communications corrupt good manners." (1 Corinthians 15:33 KJV)
3. Environmental Factors
    - Recognize how an unsupportive environment or lack of resources can hinder progress.
    - Scripture: "The Lord is my shepherd; I shall not want." (Psalm 23:1 KJV)

Overcoming External Barriers

1. Seek God's Guidance
    - Encourage youth to seek God's guidance in overcoming external barriers.
    - Scripture: "Trust in the Lord with all thine heart, and lean not unto thine own understanding. In all thy ways acknowledge him, and he shall direct thy paths." (Proverbs 3:5-6 KJV)
2. Build a Supportive Community
    - Foster connections with positive role models and supportive peers.
    - Scripture: "And let us consider one another to provoke unto love and to good works." (Hebrews 10:24 KJV)
3. Develop Resilience
    - Teach resilience and perseverance in the face of external challenges.

- Scripture: "I can do all things through Christ which strengtheneth me." (Philippians 4:13 KJV)

Exercise

1. Barrier Mapping: Have youth map their external barriers and brainstorm ways to overcome them.
2. Support Network Identification: Help youth identify supportive individuals who can provide encouragement and guidance.

Energy Drainers

Energy drainers are activities, habits, or situations that sap energy and focus, making it difficult to stay motivated and productive.

Identifying Energy Drainers

1. Unhealthy Habits
   - Recognize habits that drain energy, such as poor sleep, unhealthy eating, and lack of exercise.
   - Scripture: "Know ye not that ye are the temple of God, and that the Spirit of God dwelleth in you?" (1 Corinthians 3:16 KJV)
2. Time Wasters
   - Identify activities that consume time without providing value, such as excessive screen time or procrastination.
   - Scripture: "Redeeming the time, because the days are evil." (Ephesians 5:16 KJV)

3. Negative Thought Patterns
    o Address negative thinking and self-doubt that drain emotional and mental energy.
    o Scripture: "For as he thinketh in his heart, so is he." (Proverbs 23:7 KJV)

Overcoming Energy Drainers

1. Adopt Healthy Habits
    o Encourage healthy lifestyle choices that boost energy and well-being.
    o Scripture: "I will both lay me down in peace, and sleep: for thou, Lord, only makest me dwell in safety." (Psalm 4:8 KJV)
2. Manage Time Wisely
    o Teach time management skills and prioritization of essential tasks.
    o Scripture: "To everything there is a season, and a time to every purpose under the heaven." (Ecclesiastes 3:1 KJV)
3. Cultivate Positive Thinking
    o Promote positive thinking and affirmations based on God's Word.
    o Scripture: "Finally, brethren, whatsoever things are true, whatsoever things are honest, whatsoever things are just, whatsoever things are pure, whatsoever things are lovely, whatsoever things are of good report; if there be any virtue, and if there be any praise, think on these things." (Philippians 4:8 KJV)

Exercise

1. Energy Audit: Have youth audit their daily activities to identify energy drainers and create a plan to reduce or eliminate them.
2. Positive Affirmation Cards: Create cards with positive affirmations and scriptures to encourage positive thinking.

Obedience

Obedience to God's Word is crucial for navigating obstacles and staying on the right path. It involves aligning actions with biblical principles and trusting God's direction.

Importance of Obedience

1. Aligning with God's Will
   o Obedience ensures that actions align with God's will and purpose.
   o Scripture: "If ye love me, keep my commandments." (John 14:15 KJV)
2. Receiving God's Blessings
   o God's blessings often follow obedience to His commands.
   o Scripture: "Blessed are they that hear the word of God, and keep it." (Luke 11:28 KJV)
3. Demonstrating Faith
   o Obedience is a demonstration of faith and trust in God.

- Scripture: "But be ye doers of the word, and not hearers only, deceiving your selves." (James 1:22 KJV)

Practicing Obedience

1. Study and Apply God's Word
   - Encourage regular Bible study and application of biblical principles.
   - Scripture: "Thy word is a lamp unto my feet and a light unto my path." (Psalm 119:105 KJV)
2. Pray for Guidance
   - Teach youth to pray for guidance and strength to obey God's commands.
   - Scripture: "If any of you lack wisdom, let him ask of God, that giveth to all men liberally, and upbraideth not; and it shall be given him." (James 1:5 KJV)
3. Live with Integrity
   - Emphasize the importance of living with integrity and honesty.
   - Scripture: "Providing for honest things, not only in the sight of the Lord but also in the sight of men." (2 Corinthians 8:21 KJV)

Exercise

1. Scripture Application: Have the youth select a scripture related to obedience and plan to apply it daily.

2. Obedience Journals: Encourage youth to keep journals documenting their efforts to obey God's Word and the outcomes they experience.

Conclusion

This week, you have learned how to help youth identify and overcome external barriers and energy drainers and the importance of obedience to God's Word. By guiding them in these areas, you provide them with the spiritual and practical tools to navigate challenges and remain steadfast in their journey.

Next week, we will focus on internal barriers and strategies for getting past these barriers, equipping youth with the insights and skills needed to overcome inner obstacles and stay aligned with their vision and mission.

Week 8: Obstacles - Internal Barriers and Getting Past the Barriers

Introduction

Welcome to the final week of our course on Biblical Empowerment for Youth. This week, we will focus on identifying and overcoming internal barriers. These obstacles come from within and can hinder personal and spiritual growth. We will also explore strategies for getting past these barriers using biblical principles. By the end of this week, you will be equipped to help youth recognize and address their internal struggles, enabling them to move forward with confidence and faith.

Internal Barriers

Internal barriers are obstacles that originate from within a person, such as negative thought patterns, fear, lack of self-esteem, and spiritual doubts. These barriers can be more challenging to identify and overcome because they often require introspection and a deep reliance on God.

Identifying Internal Barriers

1. Negative Thought Patterns
   - Understand how negative self-talk and limiting beliefs can hinder progress.
   - Scripture: "For as he thinketh in his heart, so is he." (Proverbs 23:7 KJV)
2. Fear and Anxiety
   - Recognize how fear and anxiety can paralyze action and prevent growth.

- Scripture: "For God hath not given us the spirit of fear; but of power, and love, and a sound mind." (2 Timothy 1:7 KJV)
3. Lack of Self-Esteem
    - Identify feelings of unworthiness and low self-esteem that can undermine confidence.
    - Scripture: "I will praise thee; for I am fearfully and wonderfully made: marvelous are thy works; and that my soul knoweth right well." (Psalm 139:14 KJV)
4. Spiritual Doubts
    - Address doubts about faith, purpose, and God's promises.
    - Scripture: "And straightway the father of the child cried out, and said with tears, Lord, I believe; help thou mine unbelief." (Mark 9:24 KJV)

Overcoming Internal Barriers

1. Renewing the Mind
    - Encourage the renewal of the mind through God's Word to combat negative thoughts.
    - Scripture: "And be not conformed to this world: but be ye transformed by the renewing of your mind, that ye may prove what is that good, and acceptable, and perfect, will of God." (Romans 12:2 KJV)
2. Trusting in God's Promises
    - Teach youth to trust God's promises and release fear and anxiety.
    - Scripture: "Casting all your care upon him; for he careth for you." (1 Peter 5:7 KJV)

3. Building Self-Esteem in Christ
    o Help youth build their self-esteem based on their identity in Christ.
    o Scripture: "But ye are a chosen generation, a royal priesthood, a holy nation, a peculiar people; that ye should shew forth the praises of him who hath called you out of darkness into his marvelous light." (1 Peter 2:9 KJV)
4. Strengthening Faith
    o Address spiritual doubts by strengthening faith through prayer and study.
    o Scripture: "So then faith cometh by hearing, and hearing by the word of God." (Romans 10:17 KJV)

Exercise

1. Thought Journal: Have youth keep a journal to record and counteract negative thoughts with positive, biblical truths.
2. Affirmation List: Create a list of affirmations based on scriptures that reinforce self-worth and God's promises.

Getting Past the Barriers

Once internal barriers are identified, developing strategies to move past them is essential. This involves a combination of spiritual practices, support systems, and practical steps.

Strategies for Overcoming Internal Barriers

1. Prayer and Meditation

- o Encourage regular prayer and meditation on God's Word for strength and clarity.
- o Scripture: "Be careful with nothing, but in everything by prayer and supplication with thanksgiving let your requests be made known unto God." (Philippians 4:6 KJV)

2. Accountability Partners
   - o Foster relationships with accountability partners who provide support and encouragement.
   - o Scripture: "Iron sharpeneth iron; so a man sharpeneth the countenance of his friend." (Proverbs 27:17 KJV)

3. Setting Realistic Goals
   - o Help youth set realistic and achievable goals that build confidence and momentum.
   - o Scripture: "The steps of a good man are ordered by the Lord: and he delighteth in his way." (Psalm 37:23 KJV)

4. Celebrating Small Victories
   - o Encourage the celebration of small victories to build confidence and maintain motivation.
   - o Scripture: "Rejoice in the Lord always: and again I say, Rejoice." (Philippians 4:4 KJV)

Exercise

1. Prayer Circle: Form a prayer circle where youth can pray for each other's internal struggles and share encouraging scriptures.
2. Victory Log: Have youth keep a log of their victories, no matter how small, to track their progress and celebrate successes.

## Conclusion

This week, you have learned how to help youth identify and overcome internal barriers that hinder their progress. By recognizing these obstacles and applying biblical principles, youth can develop the resilience and faith needed to move forward confidently.

Throughout this course, we have explored various aspects of Biblical Empowerment, from awareness and vision to strategy and action and overcoming obstacles. Each element is crucial in guiding youth towards fulfilling their God-given potential. As you continue to support and mentor the youth, remember to rely on God's wisdom and strength, encouraging them to do the same.

## Overall Course Conclusion

In conclusion, Biblical Empowerment for Youth is a comprehensive approach to helping young people grow spiritually, emotionally, and personally. By focusing on God's Word, Jesus' teachings, the Holy Spirit, the Full Body of Armor, and the supportive community of believers, you can guide youth through the stages of change and help them overcome obstacles with faith and resilience. Remember to continuously apply these principles as you lead by example, fostering an environment where youth can thrive and fulfill their divine purpose.

# Biblical Resilience and Coping Skills Training Manual

## Course Overview

This 8-week course provides participants with biblical principles and strategies from the Bible's King James Version (KJV) for building resilience and effectively coping with life's challenges. Each week emphasizes a different aspect of developing spiritual strength.

Week 1: Foundations in God's Word and Jesus' Teachings

Objectives:

- Study scriptures that emphasize God's promises and faithfulness under challenging times.
- Discuss Jesus' teachings on endurance, faith, and overcoming adversity.

Key Concepts:

- God's Word is the foundation for resilience (Psalm 119:105 KJV: "Thy word is a lamp unto my feet and a light unto my path.")
- Jesus' teachings on perseverance and trusting God (Matthew 6:25-34, John 16:33)

Activities:

- Memorize scriptures on God's promises (e.g., Jeremiah 29:11 KJV).
- Reflect on biblical accounts of resilience (e.g., Job, Joseph, Paul).

- Discuss applying Jesus' teachings to current challenges.

Week 2: Empowerment through the Holy Spirit and Full Armor of God

Objectives:

- Explore the Holy Spirit's guidance and empowerment (John 14:16-17 KJV, Acts 1:8 KJV).
- Learn about the Full Armor of God for spiritual warfare (Ephesians 6:10-18 KJV).

Key Concepts:

- The Holy Spirit is our helper and comforter (John 14:26 KJV).
- We are putting on the whole armor for protection and strength (Ephesians 6:11 KJV).

Activities:

- Pray for the Holy Spirit's empowerment.
- Memorize the armor pieces and their spiritual significance.
- Role-play is standing firm using the armor of God.

Week 3: Support from God's Angels and Faith Community

Objectives:

- Examine biblical accounts of angelic protection (Psalm 91:11 KJV, Daniel 6 KJV).

- Discuss the faith community's role in support (Hebrews 10:24-25 KJV, Galatians 6:2 KJV).

Key Concepts:

- God's angels are ministering spirits (Hebrews 1:14 KJV).
- The importance of Christian fellowship and accountability (Proverbs 27:17 KJV).

Activities:

- Study angelic encounters in the Bible (e.g., Genesis 16, Daniel 3).
- Share testimonies of God's protection.
- Identify supportive faith community members.

Week 4: Building a Strong Belief System

Objectives:

- Explore scriptures on steadfast belief (Hebrews 11 KJV, James 1:5-8 KJV).
- Identify help systems: prayer, mentors, counseling, etc.

Key Concepts:

- Unwavering faith in God's promises (Numbers 23:19 KJV).
- We are utilizing available spiritual and practical help (James 5:16 KJV).

Activities:

- Affirm core beliefs rooted in Scripture.
- Learn to express doubts/fears and seek godly counsel.
- Practice petitioning God for wisdom and strength (James 1:5 KJV).

Week 5: Obedience and Trusting God's Safety

Objectives:

- Study the blessings of obedience (Deuteronomy 28:1-14 KJV, John 14:21 KJV).
- Discuss trusting God's protection (Psalm 91 KJV, Proverbs 18:10 KJV).

Key Concepts:

- Obedience leads to blessings and security (Deuteronomy 28:1-2 KJV).
- God is our refuge and fortress in troubles (Psalm 91:2 KJV).

Activities:

- Examine biblical accounts of God's protection through obedience (e.g., Noah, Daniel).
- Identify areas for growth in obedience and trust.
- Develop practical obedience goals.

Week 6: Goal Setting, Taking Action, and Perseverance

Objectives:

- Set SMART goals aligned with God's will (Philippians 3:14 KJV).
- Discuss persevering through challenges (James 1:2-4 KJV, Romans 5:3-5 KJV).

Key Concepts:

- Prayerfully setting goals and taking decisive action (Proverbs 16:3 KJV).
- Persevering in faith produces spiritual growth (Romans 5:3-4 KJV).

Activities:

- Write SMART goals for spiritual development.
- Study biblical examples of perseverance (e.g., Noah, Abraham, Jesus).
- Partner with an accountability buddy to encourage perseverance.

Week 7: Overcoming External Barriers and Energy Drainers

Objectives:

- Identify external barriers (e.g., societal pressures, unhealthy relationships).
- Discuss energy drainers and renewing strength (Isaiah 40:28-31 KJV).

Key Concepts:

- We are overcoming the world's influence through obedience (1 John 5:4 KJV).
- I find rest and renewal in God's presence (Matthew 11:28-30 KJV).

Activities:

- Evaluate external influences and set necessary boundaries.
- Practice spiritual disciplines to renew strength (e.g., prayer, worship, Scripture).
- Discuss practical ways to conserve energy for what matters.

Week 8: Overcoming Internal Barriers

Objectives:

- Understand internal barriers (doubts, fears, sin patterns).
- Discuss renewing the mind (Romans 12:2 KJV, Philippians 4:8 KJV).

Key Concepts:

- I am overcoming sinful tendencies through the Spirit's power (Galatians 5:16 KJV).
- I am renewing thoughts and perspectives according to God's truth (2 Corinthians 10:5 KJV).

Activities:

- Identify and confess internal barriers hindering growth.
- Practice replacing negative thoughts with biblical truth.
- Develop accountability for areas of spiritual struggle.

By completing this comprehensive 8-week course, participants will gain a biblical foundation from the KJV and practical tools to cultivate resilience, cope with adversity, and experience spiritual transformation through the power of God's Word and the Holy Spirit.

# Course: Biblical Resiliency and Coping Skills

## Course Overview

**Course Title:** Biblical Resiliency and Coping Skills

**Overview:** The "Biblical Resilience and Coping Skills" course is designed to provide participants with foundational biblical principles and practical strategies from the King James Version (KJV) of the Bible for developing resilience and effectively managing life's challenges. Over eight weeks, participants will explore various aspects of spiritual fortitude, drawing strength and wisdom from scripture to navigate and overcome adversity.

Course Objectives:

- Week 1: Establish a solid foundation in God's Word and Jesus' teachings on perseverance and faith.
- Week 2: Gain empowerment through the Holy Spirit and understand the Full Armor of God for spiritual warfare.
- Week 3: Learn about the support God's angels provided and the importance of the faith community.
- Week 4: Build a robust belief system rooted in unwavering faith and utilize available spiritual and practical support systems.
- Week 5: Understand the blessings of obedience and the security of trusting God's protection.
- Week 6: Develop skills in setting and achieving SMART goals aligned with God's will, and learn the value of perseverance.

- Week 7: Identify and overcome external barriers and energy drainers, finding renewal in God's presence.
- Week 8: Address and conquer internal barriers such as doubts, fears, and sin patterns, renewing the mind with God's truth.

Key Features:

- Scripture-Based Learning: Study and memorize key scriptures emphasizing resilience and coping mechanisms.
- Practical Activities: Engage in reflective activities, group discussions, role-playing, and practical exercises to apply biblical teachings to everyday life.
- Community Support: Foster a supportive environment through faith-based community interactions and accountability partnerships.
- Spiritual Growth: Enhance spiritual growth by developing a deeper understanding of biblical principles and their application in building resilience.

Target Audience: This course is ideal for individuals seeking to strengthen their faith, build resilience, and develop practical coping skills through a biblical framework. Whether facing personal challenges or looking to support others, participants will find valuable insights and tools to navigate life's difficulties with spiritual strength and confidence.

Outcome: By the end of this 8-week course, participants will be equipped with a robust biblical foundation and practical tools to cultivate resilience, manage adversity, and experience profound spiritual transformation through the power of God's Word and the Holy Spirit.

Biblical Example: Job

1. Name: Job

2. Story Overview:

The job was a blameless and upright man who faced severe trials orchestrated by Satan to test his faithfulness to God.

3. Experiences:

Despite losing his wealth, children, and health, Job remained steadfast in his faith and integrity.

4. Spiritual Connection and Overcoming Barriers:

Job maintained a deep spiritual connection with God throughout his suffering, never cursing God despite immense hardship. His resilience stemmed from unwavering faith in God's sovereignty.

5. The Role of the Devil:

Satan played a pivotal role in Job's trials, aiming to prove that Job would curse God if everything were taken away from him.

6. Combating Through Prayer and Scriptures (KJV Only):

Job prayed fervently and wrestled with God in his anguish, ultimately finding solace in God's wisdom and sovereignty.

- Scripture: "Though he slays me, yet will I trust in him: but I will maintain mine own ways before him." (Job 13:15 KJV)

Conclusion

This course has equipped you with biblical insights and practical strategies for fostering resilience and coping skills based on God's Word. By grounding ourselves and the youth we support in biblical teachings, relying on the Holy Spirit's guidance, nurturing supportive relationships, and practicing obedience and trust in God's safety, we can navigate life's challenges with faith and strength. As you continue to mentor and guide youth, may you inspire them to cultivate resilience and trust in God's unfailing promises, just as Job exemplified in the face of adversity.

Week 1: Awareness - The Stages of Change, Satisfaction Assessment, Circumstances, World Views, God's Words, Belief System

Introduction:

Welcome to Week 1 of our course on Biblical Resiliency and Coping Skills! This week, we will focus on understanding the stages of change, conducting a satisfaction assessment, examining our circumstances through biblical perspectives, shaping our worldview based on God's Word, and strengthening our belief system.

Objectives:

- Explore the Stages of Change: We will delve into how individuals navigate through stages of change in their spiritual journey, drawing insights from biblical examples such as transformation and growth in faith.
- Conduct a Satisfaction Assessment: Participants will reflect on different areas of their lives—spiritual, emotional, and practical—to evaluate satisfaction levels and identify areas for improvement with God's guidance.
- Evaluate Circumstances Biblically: We will learn to view life's circumstances, both challenging and favorable, through the lens of God's promises and sovereignty, fostering a deeper trust in His plans.
- Shape World Views with God's Word: Discussions will center on how God's Word is the foundation for our worldview, influencing our understanding of ourselves, others, and the world around us.

- Strengthen Belief Systems: Through scriptural exploration and personal reflection, participants will strengthen their belief in God's faithfulness, His promises, and the relevance of these beliefs in daily life.

The Stages of Change

Understanding the stages of change is crucial in our spiritual growth and resilience journey. Just as we experience various stages in physical development, our spiritual lives also go through stages that shape our relationship with God and our ability to cope with life's challenges. Here is a breakdown of these stages and how they apply to our spiritual journey:

1. Precontemplation

- Description: In this stage, individuals may still need to recognize a need for change. They may be unaware or unwilling to acknowledge a problem or an area in their spiritual life that needs attention.
- Spiritual Application: This stage often involves moments of introspection or external influences that prompt individuals to consider their spiritual journey. It may be when individuals are not actively seeking God or may be distant from Him.

2. Contemplation

- Description: Individuals in this stage are aware of a problem or an area for improvement in their spiritual life. They are considering making changes but have yet to commit to taking action.
- Spiritual Application: Contemplation in a spiritual context often involves seeking understanding through prayer, meditation on scripture, or seeking guidance from mentors or spiritual leaders. It is a time of introspection and weighing the costs and benefits of change.

3. Preparation

- Description: Individuals actively plan and prepare for change in the preparation stage. They may start taking small steps towards spiritual growth, such as regular prayer, attending church more often, or seeking out opportunities for spiritual learning.
- Spiritual Application: Preparation involves intentionally deepening one's relationship with God. This may include setting spiritual goals, identifying areas of weakness or temptation, and seeking accountability through fellowship with other believers.

4. Action

- Description: Specific, overt changes in behavior characterize the action stage. Individuals in this stage actively implement their plans for spiritual growth and make tangible efforts to overcome challenges and grow closer to God.

- Spiritual Application: Action involves committing to regular spiritual disciplines, such as daily prayer and scripture reading, engaging in acts of service, and actively participating in the church's life. It is a time of significant personal investment in one's spiritual journey.

## 5. Maintenance

- Description: Maintenance involves sustaining the changes made during the action stage over the long term. Individuals in this stage work to prevent relapse and grow spiritually, even when faced with challenges or temptations.
- Spiritual Application: Maintenance requires an ongoing commitment to spiritual disciplines and growth. It involves staying connected to God through consistent prayer and study of His Word, maintaining accountability with fellow believers, and seeking guidance and strength from the Holy Spirit.

## 6. Relapse

- Description: Relapse is a normal part of the change process where individuals may revert to old behaviors or patterns despite previous progress. Viewing relapse as an opportunity for renewed commitment and learning rather than a failure is essential.

- Spiritual Application: In a spiritual context, relapse may involve moments of doubt, temptation, or drifting away from God. It is a time to seek forgiveness, renew commitment to spiritual practices, and lean on God's grace for strength and restoration.

Conduct a Satisfaction Assessment

In Week 1 of our Biblical Resiliency and Coping Skills course, we conduct a Satisfaction Assessment to help participants evaluate various spiritual, emotional, and practical aspects of their lives. This assessment aims to identify areas of satisfaction, areas needing improvement, and ways to align these with God's guidance.

Objectives:

- Reflect on Different Areas: Participants will take time to introspect and evaluate their satisfaction levels in critical areas of life, including spiritual well-being, emotional health, relationships, work or studies, and personal growth.
- Identify Areas for Improvement: Through reflection and prayer, participants will identify specific areas where they feel dissatisfied or desire growth and improvement.
- Seek God's Guidance: Participants will seek God's wisdom and guidance in discerning areas that require change or adjustment, aligning their desires with His will for their lives.

Steps for the Satisfaction Assessment:

1. Prepare for Reflection: Find a quiet place and time to reflect without distractions. Have a notebook or journal ready for note-taking.
2. Evaluate Spiritual Well-being: Reflect on your relationship with God. How satisfied are you with your spiritual practices, such as prayer, Bible study, worship, and church or spiritual community involvement?
3. Assess Emotional Health: Consider your emotional state. Are there areas of stress, anxiety, or emotional challenges that are affecting your well-being? How satisfied are you with your emotional resilience and coping mechanisms?
4. Reflect on Relationships: Evaluate your relationships with family, friends, colleagues, and others. How satisfied are you with these relationships? Are there areas where you feel disconnected or need improvement?
5. Evaluate Work or Studies: Assess your satisfaction with your current job, studies, or daily responsibilities. Are you fulfilled in your work/studies, or do you need change or growth in this area?
6. Assess Personal Growth: Reflect on your personal growth and development. Are you satisfied with your progress in achieving personal goals, hobbies, or aspirations?
7. Identify Areas for Improvement: Based on your reflections, identify areas where you feel dissatisfied or need growth and improvement.

8. Seek God's Guidance: Pray and seek God's wisdom in discerning which areas to focus on for improvement. Ask for His guidance in setting goals and making changes aligned with His purposes for your life.

Scriptures for Reflection:

- Proverbs 3:5-6 - "Trust in the Lord with all thine heart; and lean not unto thine own understanding. In all thy ways acknowledge him, and he shall direct thy paths."
- Philippians 4:6-7 - "Be careful with nothing, but in everything by prayer and supplication with thanksgiving let your requests be made known unto God. Moreover, the peace of God, which passeth all understanding, shall keep your hearts and minds through Christ Jesus."
- Psalm 139:23-24 - "Search me, O God, and know my heart: try me, and know my thoughts: And see if there be any wicked way in me, and lead me in the way everlasting."
- James 1:5 - "If any of you lack wisdom, let him ask of God, that giveth to all men liberally, and upbraideth not; and it shall be given him."
- Romans 12:2 - "And be not conformed to this world: but be ye transformed by the renewing of your mind, that ye may prove what is that good, and acceptable, and perfect, will of God."

Reflection Questions:

- How does your current satisfaction level align with God's desires for your life?
- What areas do you need to surrender more fully to God's will and seek His guidance?
- How can you use your areas of satisfaction and dissatisfaction to draw closer to God and grow in faith?

Evaluate Circumstances Biblically

In Week 1 of our course on Biblical Resiliency and Coping Skills, we are focusing on learning to evaluate life's challenging and favorable circumstances through the lens of God's promises and sovereignty. This process aims to foster a deeper trust in His plans and a strengthened resilience in facing life's ups and downs.

Objectives:

- Understand God's Promises: Participants will explore biblical promises that assure us of God's faithfulness and plans for our lives, even under challenging circumstances.
- Recognize God's Sovereignty: Through scriptural study and reflection, participants will understand God's sovereignty—His supreme authority and control over all situations.
- Develop Trust in God's Plans: Participants will learn to trust that God works all things together for good for those who love Him (Romans 8:28 KJV),

even when circumstances seem challenging or unclear.

Steps to Evaluate Circumstances Biblically:

1. Identify Challenging Circumstances: Reflect on recent challenges or difficulties you have faced. Write down specific situations where you have felt overwhelmed or uncertain.
2. Explore Relevant Scriptures: Look up and meditate on scriptures that speak to God's promises and sovereignty under challenging times. Examples include:
   o Psalm 46:1 KJV - "God is our refuge and strength, a very present help in trouble."
   o Isaiah 41:10 KJV - "Fear thou not; for I am with thee: be not dismayed; for I am thy God: I will strengthen thee; yea, I will help thee; yea, I will uphold thee with the right hand of my righteousness."
   o Jeremiah 29:11 KJV - "For I know the thoughts that I think toward you, saith the Lord, thoughts of peace, and not of evil, to give you an expected end."
   o Romans 8:28 KJV - "And we know that all things work together for good to them that love God, to them who are the called according to his purpose."
3. Reflect on God's Faithfulness: Consider past instances where God has been faithful to you or others. How did He work through challenging circumstances for good? Share these reflections with a trusted friend or mentor.

4. Apply Biblical Principles: Apply the principles from these scriptures to your current challenges. Trust in God's promises and sovereignty as you face difficulties, knowing He is with you and has a purpose for every situation.
5. Pray for Guidance: Spend prayer, surrendering your circumstances to God and asking Him to guide you. Seek His wisdom and strength to navigate challenges with faith and resilience.

Scriptures for Reflection:

- Psalm 46:10 KJV - "Be still, and know that I am God: I will be exalted among the heathen, I will be exalted in the earth."
- Isaiah 40:31 KJV - "But they that wait upon the Lord shall renew their strength; they shall mount up with wings as eagles; they shall run, and not be weary; and they shall walk, and not faint."
- Romans 15:13 KJV - "Now the God of hope fill you with all joy and peace in believing, that ye may abound in hope, through the power of the Holy Ghost."

Reflection Questions:

- How can viewing challenging circumstances through God's promises and sovereignty strengthen your faith and resilience?
- In what ways can you actively trust God's plans for your life, even when circumstances seem complex or uncertain?

- How has God's faithfulness in past situations influenced your perspective on current challenges?

Shape World Views with God's Word

Week 1 of our Biblical Resiliency and Coping Skills course focuses on shaping our worldviews with God's Word. Discussions will center on how the Bible is the foundation for understanding ourselves, others, and the world, influencing our perspectives and actions.

Objectives:

- Understand Biblical Worldview: Participants will explore how God's Word provides a framework for viewing life, guiding our beliefs and values.
- Apply Scriptures to Life: Discussions will encourage participants to apply biblical teachings daily, fostering a deeper connection between faith and worldview.
- Discuss Practical Examples: Participants will examine how biblical principles can shape responses to various situations and challenges through examples and case studies.

Topics for Discussion:

1. Foundation of Biblical Worldview: Discuss the importance of having a worldview rooted in God's Word. How does this differ from secular or cultural worldviews?
2. Impact on Self-Identity: Explore scriptures that address our identity in Christ and how knowing

God's Word shapes our understanding of who we are.

3. Understanding Others: Reflect on scriptures emphasizing love, compassion, and understanding towards others, even those with different beliefs.
4. View of the World: Discuss biblical perspectives on the world's fallen nature and God's redemptive plan for creation.

Scriptures for Reflection:

- Psalm 119:105 KJV - "Thy word is a lamp unto my feet and a light unto my path."
- Proverbs 3:5-6 KJV - "Trust in the Lord with all thine heart, and lean not unto thine own understanding. In all thy ways acknowledge him, and he shall direct thy paths."
- John 17:17 KJV - "Sanctify them through thy truth: thy word is truth."
- 2 Timothy 3:16-17 KJV - "All scripture is given by inspiration of God, and is profitable for doctrine, for reproof, for correction, for instruction in righteousness: That the man of God may be perfect, thoroughly furnished unto all good works."

Discussion Questions:

- How does God's Word shape your beliefs and values?
- Can you share an example of a biblical principle that has influenced how you view a particular aspect of life or your decision?

- How can we apply biblical teachings to everyday situations to maintain a consistent worldview?

Strengthen Belief Systems

Week 1 of our Biblical Resiliency and Coping Skills course focuses on strengthening belief systems through scriptural exploration and personal reflection. Participants will delve into God's faithfulness, His promises, and the relevance of these beliefs in daily life.

Objectives:

- Explore God's Faithfulness: Participants will study scriptures highlighting God's faithfulness throughout history and personal experiences.
- Embrace His Promises: Through reflection and discussion, participants will deepen their trust in God's promises as relevant and applicable to their daily challenges.
- Apply Beliefs to Life: Discussions and personal reflections will help participants apply their strengthened beliefs to everyday situations, fostering resilience and faith.

Biblical Exploration:

1. God's Faithfulness: Study passages that illustrate God's faithfulness in fulfilling His promises. Reflect on how these accounts encourage trust in God's character.
   - Lamentations 3:22-23 KJV - "It is of the Lord's mercies that we are not consumed

because his compassions fail not. They are
new every morning: great is thy
faithfulness."

- o Deuteronomy 7:9 KJV - "Know therefore
  that the Lord thy God, he is God, the faithful
  God, which keepeth covenant and mercy
  with them that love him and keep his
  commandments to a thousand generations."
- o Hebrews 10:23 KJV - "Let us hold fast the
  profession of our faith without wavering;
  (for he is faithful that promised;)"

2. God's Promises: Discuss specific promises in
   Scripture and how they provide hope and guidance
   in challenging times.

   - o Philippians 4:19 KJV - "But my God shall
     supply all your need according to his riches
     in glory by Christ Jesus."
   - o Isaiah 41:10 KJV - "Fear thou not; for I am
     with thee: be not dismayed; for I am thy
     God: I will strengthen thee; yea, I will help
     thee; yea, I will uphold thee with the right
     hand of my righteousness."
   - o Matthew 11:28 KJV - "Come unto me, all ye
     that labor and are heavily laden, and I will
     give you rest."

3. Application to Daily Life: Discuss how these beliefs
   in God's faithfulness and promises impact decision-
   making, attitudes, and responses to challenges.

   - o Share personal experiences where relying on
     God's promises has brought peace or
     resolution under challenging circumstances.

- Brainstorm ways to integrate these beliefs into daily routines and interactions with others.

Reflection Questions:

- How has God demonstrated His faithfulness in your life or the lives of others you know?
- Which promises of God resonate most with you? Why?
- In what practical ways can you apply your strengthened beliefs in God's faithfulness and promises to your daily life?

Week 2: Awareness - Passions, Personality, Strengths, Spiritual Gifts, God's Help

In Week 2 of our course on Biblical Resiliency and Coping Skills, we deeply understand ourselves—our passions, personality traits, strengths, spiritual gifts, and how God helps us utilize these for His purpose.

Objectives:

- Explore Passions: Participants will identify their passions and interests, considering how these align with God's purposes.
- Understand Personality: Through personality assessments and biblical insights, participants will gain clarity on their unique personalities and how these can be leveraged for God's kingdom.
- Discover Spiritual Gifts: Participants will explore spiritual gifts outlined in Scripture, recognizing how

they empower them to serve God and others effectively.

- Acknowledge God's Help: Reflect on scriptures demonstrating God's role in guiding, supporting, and empowering individuals to fulfill their purpose.

Identifying Passions

Understanding our passions is essential as we align our lives with God's calling, finding greater fulfillment in His purposes.

Scriptures for Reflection:

- Psalm 37:4 KJV: "Delight thyself also in the Lord, and he shall give thee the desires of thine heart."

  This verse encourages us to find our delight and joy in the Lord. As we draw closer to Him, our desires align more closely with His will. When our passions are rooted in God's desires for us, He promises to fulfill them, leading to a life of purpose and satisfaction.

- 1 Corinthians 10:31 KJV "Whether therefore ye eat, or drink, or whatsoever ye do, do all to the glory of God."

  This verse reminds us that everything we do should bring glory to God. Our passions should not be self-centered but should ultimately glorify Him. By aligning our passions with God's will, we ensure that our pursuits are meaningful and impactful according to His purposes.

Discussion Points:

1.  Alignment with God's Will: How can we discern whether our passions align with God's calling for our lives?
2.  Impact on Daily Choices: How can we integrate our passions into our daily lives to honor God?
3.  Balancing Desires: How do we balance pursuing our passions and ensuring they align with God's Word and His plans for us?

Application:

*   Reflect on your current passions and interests. How do you see them aligning with God's purposes?
*   Consider instances where you have experienced God's guidance or redirection regarding your passions. Share these moments with others for encouragement and insight.

Understanding Personality

Exploring our personalities through biblical insights and assessments helps us recognize how God uniquely equips us to serve Him effectively.

Scriptures for Reflection:

- 1 Samuel 16:7 KJV "But the Lord said unto Samuel, Look not on his countenance, or the height of his stature; because I have refused him: for the Lord seeth not as man seeth; for man looketh on the outward appearance, but the Lord looketh on the heart."

  This verse reminds us that God values the inner qualities of the heart over external appearances. It encourages us to develop godly character traits that align with His purposes rather than being swayed by superficial judgments.

- Romans 12:6-8 KJV "Having then gifts differing according to the grace that is given to us, whether prophecy, let us prophesy according to the proportion of faith; Or ministry, let us wait on our ministering: or he that teacheth, on teaching; Or he that exhorteth, on exhortation: he that giveth, let him do it with simplicity; he that ruleth, with diligence; he that showeth mercy, with cheerfulness."

  These verses highlight the diversity of spiritual gifts given by God to His people. Each gift corresponds to different personality traits and abilities, emphasizing the importance of using them faithfully and effectively for the edification of the body of Christ.

Discussion Points:

1. God's Perspective on Personality: How does God view our personalities compared to how society often perceives them?
2. Examples from Scripture: Discuss biblical characters like David and Peter, highlighting their personality traits (e.g., bravery, boldness) and how they were used in their service to God.
3. Identifying Our Strengths: Reflect on personal strengths and how they can be used to glorify God and serve others effectively.

Application:

- Take time to reflect on your personality traits. How do these traits reflect God's unique design for you?
- Consider leveraging your strengths and spiritual gifts in your personal life, church community, or workplace to honor God and bless others.

Identifying Strengths

Recognizing our strengths is crucial for effective service and ministry, empowering us to fulfill God's purposes confidently.

Scriptures for Reflection:

- Philippians 4:13 KJV says, "I can do all things through Christ which strengtheneth me."

This verse reminds us that Christ empowers our abilities and strengths. When we rely on Him, He equips us to accomplish tasks and serve others beyond our capabilities.

- Ephesians 2:10 KJV: "For we are his workmanship, created in Christ Jesus unto good works, which God hath before ordained that we should walk in them."

This verse emphasizes that God has uniquely crafted us for specific purposes and good works. Recognizing our strengths allows us to walk confidently in the path God has ordained for us, serving Him and others effectively.

Discussion Points:

1. Discovering Personal Strengths: How can we identify and acknowledge our spiritual and practical strengths?
2. Using Strengths for God's Glory: Discuss examples from your life or Scripture where individuals used their strengths to serve God and impact others.
3. Balancing Humility and Confidence: How can we maintain humility while acknowledging and utilizing our strengths for God's kingdom?

Application:

- Reflect on your strengths, considering both natural abilities and spiritual gifts. How do these strengths align with opportunities for service and ministry?

- Share personal stories or testimonies where recognizing and using your strengths has led to meaningful service or ministry impact.

Discovering Spiritual Gifts

Exploring spiritual gifts as outlined in Scripture reveals how God uniquely equips believers for service and ministry within the body of Christ.

Scripture for Reflection:

- 1 Corinthians 12:4-11 KJV "Now there are diversities of gifts, but the same Spirit. There are differences in administrations, but they have the same Lord. Moreover, there are diversities of operations, but the same God works all in all. However, the manifestation of the Spirit is given to every man to profit withal. For to one is given by the Spirit the word of wisdom; to another the word of knowledge by the same Spirit; To another faith by the same Spirit; to another the gifts of healing by the same Spirit; To another the working of miracles; to another prophecy; to another discerning of spirits; to another divers kinds of tongues; to another the interpretation of tongues: But all these worketh that one and the selfsame Spirit, dividing to every man severally as he will."

  These verses illustrate the diversity of spiritual gifts given by the Holy Spirit for the church's edification. Each gift serves a unique purpose in fulfilling God's plan and building up the body of Christ.

Discussion Points:

1. Understanding Spiritual Gifts: What are spiritual gifts, and how do they differ from natural talents or skills?
2. Identifying Your Spiritual Gifts: How can individuals discern their spiritual gifts? Discuss practical ways to discover and develop these gifts.
3. Using Gifts for Edification: How do spiritual gifts contribute to the unity and growth of the church? Share examples of how specific gifts have impacted your local congregation or community.

Application:

- Reflect on the spiritual gifts listed in 1 Corinthians 12:4-11. Which gifts resonate with you personally, and how have you seen them manifest in your life or others?
- Consider opportunities within your church or community to use your spiritual gifts to serve others and advance God's kingdom.

God's Help in Utilizing Gifts

Reflecting on how God equips and empowers individuals through His Spirit to fulfill His purposes is foundational to understanding our role in His kingdom.

Scriptures for Reflection:

- 2 Corinthians 12:9 KJV "And he said unto me, My grace is sufficient for thee: for my strength is made perfect in weakness. Therefore, I will most gladly glory in my infirmities, that the power of Christ may rest upon me."

This verse emphasizes that God's grace and strength are sufficient for us, even in our weaknesses. Through our reliance on Him, His power is manifested, enabling us to use our gifts effectively for His glory.

- Philippians 2:13 KJV: "For it is God which worketh in you both to will and to do of his good pleasure."

This verse reminds us that God works within us, guiding our desires and actions according to His purposes. He empowers us not only to desire His will but also to carry it out in our lives.

Discussion Points:

1. Dependency on God's Grace: How does recognizing our dependence on God's grace and strength influence our approach to utilizing spiritual gifts?
2. Trusting God's Guidance: In what ways have you experienced God's guidance in using your spiritual gifts for His purposes?
3. Overcoming Weaknesses: How can God's strength be made perfect in our weaknesses? Discuss examples where individuals turned their weaknesses into strengths through God's empowerment.

Application:

- Reflect on when you felt inadequate or weak in using your spiritual gifts. How did God's grace sustain you and empower you to serve effectively?
- Consider ways to cultivate a more profound dependence on God's strength and guidance as you seek to utilize your gifts for His kingdom purposes.

Week 2 Conclusion

In Week 2, we explored the significance of understanding our passions, personalities, strengths, and spiritual gifts in light of God's calling and purposes for our lives. Through Scripture and discussion, we discovered how:

- Psalm 37:4 reassures us that when we delight ourselves in the Lord, He aligns our desires with His will, leading to fulfillment and satisfaction.
- 1 Corinthians 10:31 reminds us that all aspects of our lives, including our passions and strengths, should ultimately bring glory to God.

We also delved into the concept of spiritual gifts, as outlined in 1 Corinthians 12:4-11, recognizing that these gifts are diverse yet unified by the same Spirit, given for the common good of the body of Christ.

As we continue this journey of self-discovery and spiritual growth, let us remain steadfast in seeking God's guidance to discern and utilize our gifts effectively. May we be inspired to serve others with humility and love, knowing that God equips us uniquely to contribute to His kingdom.

In the upcoming weeks, we look forward to exploring further how these insights can deepen our relationship with God and impact our communities for His glory.

Week 3: Vision - Clarify the Vision & God's Safety

Introduction

Welcome to Week 3 of our journey together to explore biblical principles of vision and safety in God. This week, we will delve deeper into understanding how to clarify our vision according to God's purposes and find security in His unwavering protection.

Clarify the Vision

Clarifying our vision involves seeking God's guidance to understand His specific calling and purpose for our lives. Just as God had distinct plans for prophets like Jeremiah and apostles like Paul, He has a unique and meaningful plan for each of us.

- Jeremiah 1:5 KJV - "Before I formed thee in the belly I knew thee, and before thou camest forth out of the womb I sanctified thee, and I ordained thee a prophet unto the nations."

  This verse highlights God's intimate knowledge of us even before our birth, indicating His deliberate and purposeful design for each individual.

- Galatians 1:15-16 KJV - "But when it pleased God, who separated me from my mother's womb and called me by his grace, To reveal his Son in me, that I might preach him among the heathen; immediately I conferred not with flesh and blood."

Paul's testimony underscores how God's call transcends human plans and expectations, illustrating the importance of aligning our vision with God's divine purposes.

God's Safety

Understanding God's safety provides reassurance and confidence as we pursue His vision. His promises of protection and guidance offer steadfast security amidst life's challenges.

- Psalm 91:1-2 KJV - "He that dwelleth in the secret place of the most High shall abide under the shadow of the Almighty. I will say of the Lord; He is my refuge and my fortress: my God; in him will I trust."

  This passage portrays God as our ultimate refuge and fortress, where we find safety and shelter under His divine protection.

- Proverbs 3:5-6 KJV - "Trust in the Lord with all thine heart, and lean not unto thine own understanding. In all thy ways acknowledge him, and he shall direct thy paths."

  These verses encourage us to trust God, acknowledge His sovereignty over our lives, and entrust Him to lead us along His intended paths.

Discussion Points

1. Personal Vision Exploration: How can we actively discern God's vision for our lives? What practical steps can we take to align our aspirations with His divine purposes?
2. Trusting God's Protection: Share personal experiences where you have witnessed God's safety and protection in your life journey. How have these experiences strengthened your faith and reliance on God?
3. Living with Confidence: How does knowing and trusting God's promises of safety impact our daily decisions, interactions, and perspectives?

Application

- Reflect on specific instances where you have felt God's guidance and protection. How can these experiences shape your vision and actions moving forward?
- Consider how you can deepen your relationship with God through prayer, Scripture study, and seeking His guidance to clarify and align your vision with His divine purposes.

Conclusion

As we conclude Week 3, let us reaffirm our commitment to seeking God's guidance in clarifying our vision and trusting in His unfailing safety. By embracing His calling with confidence and relying on His protection, we can boldly step into the plans He has ordained for us. In the upcoming week, we will continue to explore how to live out God's vision with clarity and assurance in His unwavering care and guidance.

Week 4: Vision - Moving with the Mission & God's Protection

Introduction

Welcome to Week 4 of our biblical exploration of vision and God's provision. This week, we will focus on actively moving with God's mission for our lives while trusting in His steadfast protection and care.

Moving with the Mission

Moving with the mission involves aligning our actions and decisions with God's revealed vision for our lives. As we seek to fulfill His purposes, relying on His guidance and empowerment is crucial.

Scriptures for Reflection:

- Proverbs 16:9 KJV: "A man's heart deviseth his way: but the Lord directeth his steps."

  This verse emphasizes that while humans may make plans, God ultimately directs and establishes the course of our lives according to His divine plan.

- Psalm 32:8 KJV: "I will instruct thee and teach thee in the way which thou shalt go: I will guide thee with mine eye."

God promises personal guidance and instruction. He assures us that He will lead us along the path He has prepared, guiding our steps with His attentive care.

Examples:

1. Paul's Missionary Journeys: In the New Testament, we see the Apostle Paul's unwavering commitment to moving with God's mission. Despite facing numerous challenges and opposition, Paul continued proclaiming the Gospel, guided by God's direction. Acts 16:6-10 illustrates how the Holy Spirit prevented Paul from preaching in Asia and redirected him to Macedonia, highlighting God's specific guidance in Paul's mission.
2. David's Kingship: King David of Israel exemplifies someone who aligned his life with God's mission. From being a shepherd boy to becoming Israel's greatest king, David consistently sought God's guidance and followed His commands. Psalm 78:70-72 reflects on how God chose David, guiding him with a faithful heart and skillful hands to lead His people according to His divine purpose.

Discussion Points:

1. Personal Application: How can we discern God's specific mission or calling for our lives? Share individual experiences where God's guidance directed your decisions or actions.
2. Faithfulness Amid Challenges: Discuss obstacles Paul faced during his missionary journeys and how

he responded with faith and obedience to God's leading.

3. Trusting God's Guidance: Reflect on times when you struggled to trust God's guidance in difficult circumstances. How did relying on His direction bring clarity and peace?

Application:

- Take time to journal or pray about areas where you may need to seek God's guidance more intentionally. Ask Him to reveal His mission for you and clarify steps to take.
- Engage in conversations with fellow believers to share insights and experiences of how God's guidance has impacted your journey of faith and obedience.

God's Protection

God's protection is a comforting assurance that accompanies us as we fulfill His mission. His promises of safety and deliverance provide strength and courage in times of uncertainty and challenge.

Scriptures for Reflection:

- Psalm 121:7-8 KJV: "The Lord shall preserve thee from all evil: he shall preserve thy soul. The Lord shall preserve thy going out and coming in from this time forth, and even for evermore."

These verses affirm God's comprehensive protection over our lives, guarding us from harm and preserving our well-being now and for eternity.

- Isaiah 41:10 KJV: "Fear thou not; for I am with thee: be not dismayed; for I am thy God: I will strengthen thee; yea, I will help thee; yea, I will uphold thee with the right hand of my righteousness."

God reassures us of His presence and support, promising to strengthen and uphold us in every circumstance we face.

Examples:

1. Daniel in the Lion's Den (Daniel 6): Despite facing opposition for his faithfulness to God, Daniel continued to pray to God openly. God protected Daniel from the hungry lions, demonstrating His power and faithfulness to those who trust Him.
   o Application: This story teaches us that when we remain faithful to God and His mission, He provides protection even in the face of danger or opposition.
2. Paul's Escape from Damascus (Acts 9:23-25): When Paul faced threats to his life in Damascus, God protected him by enabling his escape through a basket lowered from a window in the city wall. This event illustrates God's intervention to safeguard His servant for future missions and purposes.
   o Application: It shows that God's protection extends to preserving His servants for

continued service and mission, even in
perilous situations.

Discussion Points:

1. Acting on God's Mission: Discuss how these
   examples demonstrate God's protection over those
   who faithfully serve Him. How does this impact our
   willingness to step out in faith for His kingdom?
2. Trusting in God's Protection: Share personal
   experiences or stories where you have witnessed
   God's protection in your life or the lives of others.
   How did these experiences deepen your trust in
   God?
3. Living Boldly: Reflect on how knowing God's
   promise of protection empowers us to live boldly
   for Him. What practical steps can we take to
   demonstrate our faith in His protective care?

Application:

- Reflect: Consider situations where you need God's
  protection and guidance. How can you trust Him
  more fully in these areas?
- Pray: Spend time in prayer, thanking God for His
  promise of protection and asking Him for strength
  to boldly fulfill His mission in your life.

Week 4 Conclusion: Moving with the Mission & God's
Protection

Throughout this week, we have explored the importance of
moving with God's mission and relying on His protection.

As we align our actions and decisions with His revealed vision for our lives, we are reminded of His sovereignty and faithfulness in guiding our steps.

Reflection on Scriptures:

- Proverbs 16:9 KJV: "A man's heart deviseth his way: but the Lord directeth his steps."

  This verse emphasizes the partnership between our planning and God's direction. It reminds us that while we may make our plans, God guides us according to His perfect will.

- Psalm 32:8 KJV: "I will instruct thee and teach thee in the way which thou shalt go: I will guide thee with mine eye."

  God promises personal guidance and instruction. He watches over us attentively, ensuring we walk the paths He has prepared for us.

Examples of God's Protection:

1. Daniel in the Lion's Den: God protected Daniel from the lions despite the threat of death because of his unwavering faith and commitment to prayer.
2. Paul's Escape from Damascus: When faced with danger, God provided a way to escape, demonstrating His protective hand over His servants.

Discussion Points:

1.  Trusting in Divine Guidance: How can we discern God's guidance in our daily decisions and actions? Share instances where God has redirected your plans for His purposes.
2.  Living with Confidence: Reflect on times when you have experienced God's protection in challenging situations. How did His faithfulness strengthen your faith?
3.  Walking in Obedience: How does God's promise of protection empower us to boldly obey His calling, even when faced with opposition or obstacles?

Application:

*   Personal Reflection: Consider areas where you need to surrender control and trust in God's guidance and protection. Ask Him to reveal His will more clearly to you.
*   Action Steps: Identify practical steps to align more closely with God's mission and rely on His protective care as you advance in faith.

Closing Thoughts:

As we conclude this week's study, let us reaffirm our commitment to moving with God's mission and trusting in His protection. Just as He guided Daniel and Paul through challenging circumstances, He continues to lead and safeguard us today. May we continue to walk boldly in His will, knowing that His plans for us are good and that He is faithful to fulfill His promises. In the upcoming week, we will delve deeper into how God equips us with His Spirit and prepares us to meet His purposes with courage and perseverance.

Week 5: Strategy and Action - Create a Strategy and the Full Body of Armor

In Week 5, we will focus on developing a strategic approach to living out our faith and understanding the importance of equipping ourselves with God's spiritual armor for protection and strength.

Create a Strategy

Developing a strategy involves planning and preparing to effectively carry God's mission into our lives. Just as a general plan for battle, we, too, must plan how to advance in our spiritual journey with purpose and clarity.

Scriptures for Reflection:

- Proverbs 19:21 KJV: "There are many devices in a man's heart; nevertheless the counsel of the Lord, that shall stand."

  This verse underscores the importance of seeking God's wisdom and guidance in planning. Despite our human ideas and schemes, the counsel of the Lord ultimately prevails and leads us on the path He has prepared for us.

- Proverbs 16:3 KJV "Commit thy works unto the Lord, and thy thoughts shall be established."

This scripture encourages us to commit our plans, actions, and thoughts to the Lord. When we surrender our strategies to Him, He directs our steps and establishes the path ahead, ensuring we walk in His will and purpose.

Examples:

1. Paul's Strategic Missionary Journeys: In Acts 13-20, we see how Paul strategically planned and executed his missionary journeys. Through prayer, fasting, and seeking God's guidance, Paul effectively spread the Gospel across various regions despite facing numerous challenges.
2. Nehemiah's Strategic Planning: Nehemiah, in Nehemiah 2-6, meticulously planned the rebuilding of Jerusalem's walls. Through prayer, he sought God's guidance and took practical steps to mobilize the people, address obstacles, and complete the project successfully.

Discussion Points:

1. The Role of Planning: Discuss why planning is essential for Christians in fulfilling God's mission. How does planning help us align with God's purposes and respond to His call effectively?
2. Seeking God's Counsel: How can we practically seek and discern God's wisdom in our strategic planning? Share personal experiences where seeking God's counsel led to clarity and direction.
3. Trusting God's Guidance: Reflect on when trusting in God's guidance and implementing strategic plans

that resulted in spiritual growth, impactful ministry, or personal transformation.

Application:

- Develop Your Spiritual Strategy: Outline a strategic plan for your spiritual journey. Include goals for prayer, Scripture study, serving others, and personal growth in Christ-likeness.
- Commitment to God's Guidance: Identify areas where you need to surrender control and seek God's counsel more intentionally. Pray for His wisdom and guidance as you implement your plans according to His will.

The Full Armor of God

Ephesians 6:10-18 KJV describes the spiritual armor that God provides for every believer. Each piece of this armor represents a crucial aspect of our spiritual readiness and protection in our faith journey.

- Belt of Truth: This represents being grounded in God's truth amidst a world of falsehoods and deception. Just as a soldier's belt holds their armor, God's truth holds together our spiritual life.
- Breastplate of Righteousness: It guards our hearts against sin and temptation, protecting our innermost being with the righteousness of Christ.
- Shoes of the Gospel of Peace: These shoes equip us to share the good news of Christ's salvation with others, enabling us to stand firm in peace even in turbulent times.

- Shield of Faith: Our faith in God's promises protects against the attacks of doubt, fear, and spiritual adversaries, enabling us to extinguish their fiery darts.
- Helmet of Salvation: This assures us of our salvation through Christ, protecting our minds from doubts and securing our hope in Him.
- Sword of the Spirit (Word of God): The Word of God is our offensive weapon, enabling us to discern truth, combat lies, and effectively engage in spiritual warfare.
- Prayer: Constant communion with God is essential for His guidance, strength, and protection. It keeps us connected to His power and wisdom.

Discussion Points:

1. Strategic Planning: Why is it crucial for Christians to have a strategic plan in their spiritual journey? How can we ensure our plans align with God's will and purposes?
2. Understanding the Armor: Discuss the significance of each piece of God's armor in daily spiritual battles. How can we actively utilize this armor to resist temptation and overcome challenges?
3. Practical Application: Share personal examples or stories where relying on God's armor (truth, righteousness, gospel, faith, salvation, Word, prayer) has protected and strengthened your faith in challenging times.

Application:

- Personal Strategy: Take intentional steps to develop a strategic plan for your spiritual growth and mission in your community. Seek God's guidance through prayer and study of Scripture to outline specific goals and actions.
- Armor Check: Reflect on how effectively you utilize each piece of God's armor in your daily life. Identify areas where you need to strengthen your reliance on His protection and adjust accordingly.

Conclusion:

As we delve into the concept of God's whole armor, let us be encouraged to actively engage in spiritual warfare with confidence in His provision and protection. By intentionally putting on each piece of God's armor and staying connected to Him through prayer, we can effectively navigate life's challenges and fulfill His purposes. May this week's focus on the armor of God equip us to stand firm in our faith, proclaim the gospel boldly, and live out God's calling with resilience and strength.

Week 6: Strategy and Action - Setting Goals, Taking Action, Moving the Process Forward

In Week 6, we delve into the practical aspects of our spiritual journey, focusing on setting goals, taking action, and persistently moving forward in faith. Just as God equips us with His armor for protection and readiness, He also calls us to engage actively in His mission through deliberate planning and faithful execution.

Setting Goals

Setting goals is a foundational aspect of our spiritual journey, guiding us toward growth, service, and alignment with God's purpose for our lives.

Proverbs 16:3 KJV
"Commit thy works unto the Lord, and thy thoughts shall be established."

This verse emphasizes the importance of committing our plans and endeavors to the Lord. When we surrender our goals to Him, He aligns our thoughts and directs our steps according to His will.

Philippians 3:13-14 KJV
"Brethren, I count not myself to have apprehended: but this one thing I do, forgetting those things which are behind, and reaching forth unto those things which are before, I press toward the mark for the prize of the high calling of God in Christ Jesus."

Paul's perspective challenges us to focus forward, setting goals that reflect our calling in Christ. It requires letting go of past mistakes and distractions and striving toward the spiritual prize and purpose God has set before us.

Examples:

1. Personal Growth: Commit to reading through a specific book of the Bible each month to deepen your understanding of God's Word.

2. Service: Set a goal to volunteer weekly at a local charity or church ministry, using your gifts to serve others in practical ways.
3. Mission: Plan to attend a missions training course to prepare for future opportunities to share the Gospel in your community or abroad.

Discussion Points:

- Aligning Goals with God's Will: Why is it crucial to align our goals with God's Word and His plans for us? How can we discern His will when setting personal and spiritual goals?
- Letting Go and Moving Forward: What are some practical steps to release past failures and focus on future goals that honor God? How does Paul's example inspire us to press on towards our calling?
- Practical Strategies: Share effective strategies for setting SMART (Specific, Measurable, Achievable, Relevant, Time-bound) goals in different areas of life. How can our goals reflect our commitment to spiritual growth and service?

Application:

- Reflect and Pray: Spend time reflecting on areas of your life where God is calling you to set new goals. Pray for clarity and wisdom in discerning His direction.
- Write Down Goals: Take the step to write down specific spiritual goals for the next month or quarter. Share these goals with a mentor or accountability partner for support.

Taking Action

Taking action is vital to our faith journey, reflecting our obedience to God's Word and our commitment to His purposes.

James 1:22 KJV
"But be ye doers of the word, and not hearers only, deceiving your own selves."

This verse reminds us that true faith is demonstrated through action. Merely hearing God's Word is insufficient; we must actively apply it through obedience and service to others.

Ephesians 2:10 KJV
"For we are his workmanship, created in Christ Jesus unto good works, which God hath before ordained that we should walk in them."

God has uniquely designed us for good works that advance His kingdom. As His redeemed children, we are called to engage in actions that align with His will and contribute to His divine plan for our lives and the world.

Examples:

1. Daily Devotion: Commit to a daily prayer and Bible study routine to deepen your relationship with God and align your actions with His Word.
2. Acts of Kindness: Look for opportunities to show kindness and compassion to those around you, reflecting the love of Christ in practical ways.

3. Service in Church: Volunteer for a ministry role within your church community, using your talents and gifts to serve others and support the church's mission.

Discussion Points:

- Obedience and Faith: Why must believers move beyond passive listening to active obedience in their faith journey? How does taking action strengthen our relationship with God?
- God's Design and Purpose: How can we discern God's specific purposes and good works He has prepared for us? Share examples of how God has used your actions to impact others for His kingdom.
- Challenges and Rewards: Discuss your challenges in taking action for God. How did these experiences deepen your faith and reliance on Him?

Application:

- Identify Action Steps: Reflect on areas where God calls you to obey His Word. Write down specific steps this week to demonstrate your faith through deeds.
- Pray for Guidance: Seek God's guidance and strength as you embark on action aligned with His purposes. Ask for His wisdom in discerning opportunities for service and obedience.

Moving the Process Forward

Moving the process forward in our spiritual journey involves trusting in God's faithfulness, persevering in faith, and continually relying on His strength to fulfill His purposes.

Philippians 1:6 KJV
"Being confident of this very thing, that he which hath begun a good work in you will perform it until the day of Jesus Christ."

This verse assures us of God's commitment to complete the work He has started in us. As we move forward, we do so with confidence in His faithfulness and His promise to bring His work to completion in our lives.

Galatians 6:9 KJV
"And let us not be weary in well doing: for in due season we shall reap if we faint not."

This encourages us to persevere in doing good and moving forward in faith, knowing that our efforts in God's service will yield fruit in His appointed time despite challenges or delays.

Examples:

1. Setting Spiritual Growth Goals: Commit to deepening your prayer life by dedicating specific times each day to prayer and journaling your reflections on God's Word.

2. Taking Action in Service: Volunteer regularly at a local shelter or community outreach program, demonstrating Christ's love through practical acts of service to those in need.
3. Moving Forward in Faith: Enroll in a missions training program to prepare for a short-term mission trip, trusting God to open doors for effectively sharing the Gospel and serving others.

Discussion Points:

- Trusting God's Timing: Why is it important to trust God's timing in our spiritual growth and service? How does patience in waiting on Him strengthen our faith?
- Overcoming Challenges: Share personal experiences of persevering through challenges while pursuing God's call. How did these experiences shape your faith and reliance on His strength?
- Celebrating Progress: Reflect on moments where you have seen God's faithfulness in moving you forward in your spiritual journey. How did these milestones encourage your faith in Him?

Application:

- Evaluate Spiritual Progress: Assess your spiritual growth goals and identify areas where you can take intentional steps to move forward in faith.
- Persist in Well-Doing: Commit to not growing weary in doing good, whether in personal spiritual

disciplines or serving others. Trust God's promise that your efforts will bear fruit in His time.

Week 6 Conclusion: Moving Forward with Purpose

Throughout Week 6, we have explored the importance of setting goals, taking action, and persisting in our spiritual journey with God. Drawing from Scripture and practical examples, we have seen how God calls us to participate in His work and actively trust His faithfulness.

Reflecting on Scripture:

- Philippians 1:6 KJV reminds us of God's commitment to complete the good work He has started in us, filling us with confidence as we move forward in His purposes.
- Galatians 6:9 KJV encourages perseverance in doing good, assuring us that our efforts in God's service will bear fruit in due time if we do not grow weary.

Discussion Highlights:

- Trusting God's Timing: We discussed why trusting God's timing is crucial in our spiritual growth and service, recognizing that His plans unfold perfectly according to His will.
- Overcoming Challenges: Many shared personal stories of overcoming challenges while pursuing God's call, demonstrating how these experiences deepen our faith and reliance on God's strength.

- Celebrating Progress: Reflecting on moments where we have witnessed God's faithfulness in moving us forward bolstered our faith and inspired us to persevere in our spiritual journey.

Application Points:

- Evaluate Progress: We evaluated our spiritual growth goals and identified areas where intentional steps can be taken to advance in faith.
- Persist in Well-Doing: Committing to not growing weary in doing well in personal spiritual disciplines and serving others, we affirmed our trust in God's promise that our efforts will yield fruit in His time.

As we conclude Week 6, let us continue to press on with purpose and determination, knowing that God goes before us, guiding our steps and empowering us to fulfill His mission. May we draw strength from His Word and the examples of faith around us, moving forward and obeying His calling on our lives.

Week 7: Obstacles - External Barriers, Energy Drainers & Obedience

Welcome to Week 7 of our journey to explore Biblical resilience and coping skills. This week, we delve into the challenges that can hinder our spiritual growth—external barriers, energy drainers, and the importance of obedience to God's Word.

Understanding External Barriers

External barriers in our spiritual journey originate from external pressures, expectations, and adversities that test our faith and commitment to God. These obstacles can take various forms, including societal norms, cultural expectations, persecution, worldly temptations, or misunderstandings from others regarding our faith.

Scripture Reflection:

Romans 12:2 KJV: "And be not conformed to this world: but be ye transformed by the renewing of your mind, that ye may prove what is that good, and acceptable, and perfect, will of God."

This verse from Romans calls us to resist conforming to the patterns and values of the world around us. Instead, it challenges us to continually renew our minds according to God's truth. By doing so, we can discern His perfect will amidst external pressures. This renewal enables us to remain steadfast in our faith and navigate challenges without compromising our beliefs.

Discussion Points:

1. Identifying External Barriers: What external influences challenge your faith journey? How do these pressures affect your spiritual growth?
2. Resisting Conformity: How can we resist conforming to worldly norms while engaging meaningfully in society? Share practical strategies

for staying true to Biblical principles in a secular world.

3. Renewing Your Mind: What practices or habits help you restore your mind according to God's truth? How does this practice strengthen your ability to discern God's will amidst external pressures?

Application:

- Evaluate External Influences: Identify specific external barriers currently affecting your spiritual journey. Reflect on how these challenges impact your faith and discernment.
- Renew Your Mind: Commit to regular practices that renew your mind according to God's Word. This may include daily scripture reading, prayer, and fellowship with other believers.
- Stand Firm: Determine areas where you need to stand firm in your faith despite external pressures. Seek God's guidance and strength to remain steadfast in His truth.

As we explore the concept of external barriers this week, may we grow in discernment, renew our minds in God's truth, and stand firm in our faith amidst worldly challenges? Through prayer and reliance on God's Word, let us overcome these obstacles and continue to walk boldly in His will.

Identifying Energy Drainers

Energy drainers are elements in our lives that deplete our spiritual vitality and hinder our growth in Christ. These activities, relationships, or mindsets distract us from focusing on God and living according to His will. Examples include sinful habits, negative influences, excessive busyness, and distractions that lead us away from nurturing our relationship with God.

Scripture Reflection:

Galatians 5:16 KJV: "This I say then, Walk in the Spirit, and ye shall not fulfill the lust of the flesh."

The verse from Galatians emphasizes the importance of walking in the Spirit. When we prioritize living according to God's Spirit, we are better equipped to discern and overcome energy drainers that tempt us to fulfill the desires of our flesh. Walking in the Spirit empowers us to maintain spiritual focus, resist distractions, and prioritize activities that align with God's purposes for our lives.

Discussion Points:

1. Identifying Energy Drainers: Reflect on specific activities, relationships, or mindsets that drain your spiritual energy. How do these drainers hinder your relationship with God?
2. Prioritizing Spiritual Growth: What strategies can you implement to prioritize spiritual growth and minimize distractions? Share practical steps to strengthen your spiritual vitality.
3. Walking in the Spirit: How does walking in the Spirit help you overcome energy drainers and live according to God's will? Share personal

experiences or examples of how spiritual focus impacts daily choices.

Application:

- Evaluate Spiritual Energy Levels: Assess which activities or relationships drain your spiritual energy. Consider reducing or eliminating these drainers to foster a deeper relationship with God.
- Set Boundaries: Establish boundaries to protect your spiritual vitality. This may involve limiting time spent on distractions or prioritizing activities that nourish your faith.
- Seek Spiritual Refreshment: Engage in practices that renew your spirit, such as prayer, worship, and studying God's Word. Commit to regular spiritual disciplines to maintain a vibrant relationship with Him.

As we explore energy drainers this week, may we grow in discernment and wisdom to prioritize activities that honor God? By walking in the Spirit and focusing on His purposes, may we overcome distractions and continue to deepen our relationship with Him.

Embracing Obedience

Obedience to God's Word is fundamental to navigating external barriers and resisting energy drainers in our spiritual journey. It requires aligning our thoughts, actions, and decisions with His divine will, even when faced with challenges or opposition.

Scripture Reflection:

1 John 5:3 KJV "For this is the love of God, that we keep his commandments: and his commandments are not grievous."

This verse from 1 John highlights the connection between love for God and obedience to His commandments. Obedience is not merely a duty but a demonstration of our love and trust in God. When we willingly obey His Word, we align ourselves with His divine plan and protect ourselves from spiritual pitfalls.

Discussion Points:

1. The Role of Obedience: Discuss why obedience to God's Word is essential for spiritual growth and resilience. How does obedience strengthen our relationship with God?
2. Challenges in Obedience: Reflect on times when obedience to God's Word was challenging. How did you overcome these challenges, and what lessons did you learn about trusting God's guidance?
3. Practical Steps Toward Obedience: Share practical strategies for cultivating obedience in daily life. How can we develop a habit of seeking and following God's will in all circumstances?

Application:

- Commitment to God's Commandments: Evaluate areas of your life where obedience to God's Word may be lacking. Pray for strength and guidance to align your actions with His teachings.

- Seeking Wisdom: Seek guidance through prayer and Scripture to discern God's will in challenging situations. Trust His promises and rely on His strength to obey faithfully.
- Accountability and Support: Partner with a trusted friend or mentor to encourage each other in obedience. Share struggles and victories in living out God's Word obediently.

As we embrace obedience this week, may we deepen our love for God by keeping His commandments. Let us rely on His grace and guidance to navigate challenges, knowing that obedience leads to spiritual growth and resilience in our faith journey.

Week 8: Obstacles - Internal Barriers and Getting Past the Barriers

In Week 8, we delve into understanding and overcoming internal barriers that hinder our spiritual growth and relationship with God. Internal barriers often originate from within ourselves—such as doubts, fears, sinful tendencies, and negative thought patterns—that can impede our progress in following Christ wholeheartedly.

Understanding Internal Barriers

Internal barriers are hindrances that originate within us, impacting our spiritual journey and relationship with God. These barriers often stem from doubts, fears, sinful habits, negative thought patterns, or unresolved emotions, preventing us from fully trusting and obeying God.

Scripture Reflection:

Psalm 139:23-24 KJV: "Search me, O God, and know my heart: try me, and know my thoughts: And see if there be any wicked way in me, and lead me in the way everlasting."

Psalm 139 invites God to search our hearts and reveal any internal barriers hindering our walk with Him. It encourages us to acknowledge these barriers and seek His guidance and grace to overcome them. By inviting God into our innermost being, we open ourselves to His transformative work that leads us on the path of everlasting life.

Biblical Examples:

1. David (Psalm 51)
After his sin with Bathsheba, David experienced profound internal barriers of guilt and shame. In Psalm 51, he pours his heart to God, acknowledging his sinful nature and seeking cleansing and renewal. Despite his internal struggles, David trusts in God's mercy and seeks restoration in his relationship.

2. Peter (Luke 22:31-34, 54-62)
Peter faced internal barriers of fear and doubt, especially during Jesus' trial and crucifixion. Despite his bold declaration of loyalty to Jesus, Peter denied Him three times out of fear. However, after Jesus' resurrection, Peter

confronts his internal barriers of guilt and shame, receiving forgiveness and restoration through Jesus' love and grace.

## 3. Paul (2 Corinthians 12:7-10)

Paul experienced an internal barrier in the form of a "thorn in the flesh," which he prayed for God to remove. However, God's response taught Paul that His grace is sufficient, even in weakness. Paul learned to rely on God's strength to overcome his limitations and continue in his ministry.

## 4. Elijah (1 Kings 19:1-18)

After a great victory over the prophets of Baal, Elijah faced internal barriers of fear and discouragement when threatened by Queen Jezebel. Despite his despair, God met Elijah in a gentle whisper, renewing his faith and commissioning him to continue his prophetic mission.

## 5. Jonah (Jonah 1-4)

Jonah faced internal barriers of disobedience and pride when God called him to preach repentance to the people of Nineveh. Instead of obeying, Jonah fled in the opposite direction. Through trials at sea and in the belly of a great fish, Jonah learned the importance of surrendering to God's will and experienced God's grace and mercy.

Discussion Points:

1. Identifying Internal Barriers: Reflect on common internal barriers such as doubts, fears, sinful habits, negative thought patterns, or unresolved emotions. How do these barriers affect our relationship with God and others?

2. Addressing Internal Barriers: Discuss strategies for recognizing and addressing internal barriers in our lives, using biblical examples like David, Peter, Paul, Elijah, and Jonah. How can their experiences guide us in seeking God's forgiveness, renewal, and restoration?
3. Trusting God's Guidance: Share examples of times when seeking God's guidance and grace has helped overcome internal barriers. How has His Word and Spirit led you toward greater spiritual freedom?

Application:

- Personal Reflection: Care your heart and identify any internal barriers hindering your relationship with God. Pray Psalm 139:23-24, inviting God to reveal areas needing His transformation.
- Spiritual Discipline: Commit to daily prayer and Scripture study to renew your mind and replace negative thought patterns with God's truth, following the examples of David, Peter, Paul, Elijah, and Jonah.
- Community Support: Seek accountability and encouragement from a trusted friend or mentor to help address and overcome internal barriers. Share insights and pray together for spiritual breakthroughs, trusting in God's faithfulness to guide and transform.

As we explore internal barriers in Week 8, may we trust God's faithfulness to guide us toward spiritual growth and freedom. Through His grace, let us embrace the journey of transformation and obedience, yielding to His loving care over our hearts and lives.

Getting Past the Barriers

In Week 8, we delve into overcoming internal barriers that hinder our spiritual growth and relationship with God. These barriers originate within us, including doubts, fears, sinful habits, negative thought patterns, and unresolved emotions. Overcoming them requires intentional effort, reliance on God's strength, and a commitment to obedience to His Word.

Scripture Reflection:

Philippians 4:13 KJV says, "I can do all things through Christ which strengtheneth me."

This verse reminds us that through Christ, we can overcome any barrier that stands in the way of our obedience and spiritual growth. His power within us enables us to press forward and conquer internal challenges.

Biblical Examples:

1. Moses (Exodus 3-4)
Moses faced internal barriers of insecurity and inadequacy when God called him to lead the Israelites out of Egypt. Despite his doubts and fears, God assured Moses of His presence and equipped him with His power to fulfill His purpose.

2. Gideon (Judges 6-8)
Gideon wrestled with internal barriers of fear and doubt
when God called him to deliver Israel from the Midianites.
Gideon overcame his uncertainties through God's guidance
and assurance and led Israel to victory, demonstrating faith
and obedience.

3. Mary Magdalene (Luke 8:1-3; John 20:11-18)
Mary Magdalene battled internal barriers of shame and
guilt due to her past sins. However, encountering Jesus
transformed her life, and she became a devoted follower
who witnessed His resurrection and proclaimed His gospel
boldly.

4. Thomas (John 20:24-29)
Thomas struggled with internal barriers of doubt regarding
Jesus' resurrection. However, encountering the risen Christ
and His wounds strengthened his faith, leading him to
declare, "My Lord and my God!"

5. Zacchaeus (Luke 19:1-10)
Zacchaeus faced internal barriers of greed and social
rejection. Upon encountering Jesus, he repented and
transformed, demonstrating the power of Christ to
overcome internal obstacles and lead to radical life change.

Discussion Points:

1. Recognizing Internal Barriers: Reflect on common
   internal barriers such as insecurity, doubt, fear,
   guilt, and sinful habits. How do these barriers
   impact our relationship with God and our ability to
   fulfill His calling?

2. Steps to Overcome Barriers: Discuss strategies from biblical examples like Moses, Gideon, Mary Magdalene, Thomas, and Zacchaeus to overcome internal barriers. How can trusting in God's promises and seeking His guidance help us move forward?
3. Embracing God's Strength: Share personal experiences or stories where relying on God's strength has enabled you to overcome internal barriers and grow spiritually. How can we encourage one another to lean on Christ's power in times of weakness?

Application:

- Personal Reflection: Identify internal barriers hindering your spiritual growth and relationship with God. Pray Philippians 4:13, asking God to strengthen and guide you in overcoming these obstacles.
- Action Steps: Develop a practical action plan to address internal barriers, such as committing to regular prayer and Scripture study, seeking accountability, and practicing forgiveness and repentance.
- Encouraging Others: Share insights and encouragement with fellow believers facing similar internal barriers. Offer support and prayer, emphasizing the transformative power of Christ's love and grace.

As we conclude Week 8, let us be encouraged by the examples of faith and obedience in Scripture. By relying on

God's strength and trusting in His promises, we can overcome internal barriers and continue to grow in our faith journey.

Overall Course Conclusion

Throughout this self-paced course on Biblical Resiliency and Coping Skills, we have explored essential principles and practices rooted in God's Word to strengthen our faith and navigate life's challenges. Each week has provided valuable insights and practical strategies to equip parents, guardians, and trusted adults in guiding youth toward a deeper relationship with God and a resilient spiritual journey.

Foundational Principles: We began by emphasizing the importance of grounding ourselves and the youth in God's Word, understanding Jesus' teachings, and relying on the empowering presence of the Holy Spirit. These foundational truths are anchors amidst life's storms, providing clarity, strength, and direction.

Equipped with Spiritual Armor: Examining the whole armor of God from Ephesians 6:10-18, we learned to clothe ourselves with truth, righteousness, the gospel of peace, faith, salvation, and the Word of God. These components defend us against spiritual attacks and empower us to boldly proclaim the gospel and live out our faith with courage.

Identifying and Utilizing Spiritual Gifts: We explored the diversity of spiritual gifts and how they are essential for building up the body of Christ. By identifying and utilizing these gifts, individually and in the community, we enhance our effectiveness in serving God and others, fulfilling our unique callings.

Strategic Planning and Action: Setting goals aligned with God's will, taking decisive action, and continually moving forward in faith were central themes in developing a proactive spiritual life. We learned the importance of perseverance and trusting God's guidance through biblical examples and practical applications.

Overcoming Obstacles: Addressing both external barriers (such as societal pressures and worldly temptations) and internal barriers (such as doubts, fears, and sinful habits), we explored how obedience to God's Word and reliance on His strength enable us to triumph over adversity and grow in spiritual maturity.

Personal Growth and Application: Throughout the course, personal reflection, prayer, and practical application were encouraged to foster spiritual growth and resilience. By applying biblical principles to daily life, participants were equipped to navigate challenges with faith, hope, and a reliance on God's promises.

Encouragement and Support: Finally, the course emphasized the importance of community, accountability, and supporting one another in the faith journey. By sharing experiences, offering encouragement, and praying for each other, participants strengthened their resolve to live out their faith authentically and courageously.

As we conclude this course, may we continue to walk in the knowledge that God is faithful to strengthen, protect, and guide us through every trial and triumph. Let us press forward with confidence, knowing that our identity and purpose are secure in Christ and that His grace is sufficient for all our needs. May we grow in resilience, deepen our trust in God, and shine His light brightly in a world that desperately needs His love and truth.

Scripture Encouragement: "Now unto him that can do exceeding abundantly above all that we ask or think, according to the power that worketh in us, Unto him be glory in the church by Christ Jesus throughout all ages, world without end. Amen." - Ephesians 3:20-21 KJV

Learnings from Biblical Figures:

1. David - A man after God's heart, David faced numerous trials, including battles against giants like Goliath and personal struggles with sin. His life teaches us about repentance, trust in God's deliverance, and the importance of genuine worship.
2. Peter - Bold and impulsive, Peter exemplifies both courage and vulnerability. His denial of Jesus underscores the human frailty we all face. However, his restoration by Christ and subsequent leadership in the early church highlight the transformative power of God's grace and forgiveness.
3. Paul - From persecutor of Christians to apostle and missionary, Paul's life is a testament to God's ability to transform hearts radically. His unwavering faith in the face of adversity, including

imprisonment and persecution, inspires perseverance and commitment to the gospel.

4. Joseph - Sold into slavery by his brothers, Joseph endured years of hardship and unjust imprisonment. However, through God's providence and Joseph's steadfast faithfulness, he became an influential leader in Egypt, ultimately reconciling with his family and exemplifying forgiveness and divine purpose.

5. Esther - Chosen as queen of Persia, Esther courageously risked her life to save her people from destruction. Her story illustrates the importance of courage, faithfulness, and trusting God's timing in fulfilling His purposes.

Course Reflection:

As we conclude, let us reflect on the lives of these biblical figures who exemplified resilience and faith amidst adversity. Their stories remind us that God is faithful and sovereign, guiding us through every challenge and using our trials for His glory and growth.

Personal Application:

Moving forward, let us apply the principles learned:

- Embrace God's Word: Ground ourselves in Scripture to discern His will and nurture our faith.
- Activate Spiritual Armor: Clothe ourselves daily with the armor of God to stand firm against spiritual attacks.

- Utilize Spiritual Gifts: Discover and utilize our spiritual gifts to serve others and build up the body of Christ.
- Navigate Obstacles: Face external and internal barriers with obedience, prayer, and reliance on God's strength.
- Grow in Resilience: Commit to continual growth in resilience, trusting in God's provision and guidance.

May this course continue to inspire and equip us to live boldly for Christ, trusting in His promises and walking confidently in His grace. As we apply these lessons, may we shine as lights in a dark world, proclaiming His love and truth to all.

Scripture Encouragement: "Now unto him that can do exceeding abundantly above all that we ask or think, according to the power that worketh in us, Unto him be glory in the church by Christ Jesus throughout all ages, world without end. Amen." - Ephesians 3:20-21 KJV

## References:

Any references to historical events, real people, or real places are used fictitiously. Names, characters, and places are products of the author's imagination.

Brief Scripture quotations marked KJV are from the King James Version(R). (1989-2022) Olive Tree Bible Reader Software, Inc. Spokane, WA: Olive Tree.